THE LIGHTER SIDE
OF A SERIOUS MISSION

THE LIGHTER SIDE
OF A SERIOUS MISSION

Kenyon H. Powers

AMBASSADOR INTERNATIONAL
GREENVILLE, SOUTH CAROLINA & BELFAST, NORTHERN IRELAND

THE LIGHTER SIDE OF A SERIOUS MISSION

Cover design & page layout by A&E Media — David Siglin

ISBN 978 1 932307 97 9

Published by the Ambassador Group

Ambassador Emerald International
427 Wade Hampton Blvd.
Greenville, SC 29609 USA
www. emeraldhouse.com

and

Ambassador Publications Ltd.
Providence House
Ardenlee Street
Belfast BT6 8QJ
Northern Ireland
www. ambassador-productions.com

The colophon is a trademark of Ambassador

This book is published in association with
Patti M. Hummel, President & Agent
The Benchmark Group LLC, Nashville, TN
benchmarkgroup1@aol.com

Cover artwork by Marina Banick

DEDICATION

I dedicate this book to you Micah, Dawson and Laurel for your willingness to grow up in another culture with patience, flexibility, and a great attitude without complaint. You made it all possible. You are a blessing to my life. I love you.

CONTENTS

PREFACE

"You should write a book!" This is what I'd been hearing for years after telling people in America about something crazy that happened to me in Ukraine. Well, after hearing this so many times, I decided to do it! Also, I really wanted to have this time in my life recorded on paper, since I haven't kept a journal all these years, plus when my mind goes, I won't be able to tell my grandchildren a thing about it! Now everybody can read all about it. All my missionary friends, who may never get around to writing their own book, can use my book to let all their family and friends know what they've experienced in Ukraine too. I'm sure most of what's in my book would also be in theirs.

Every story I've told you in this book is true. I've not changed the names to protect the innocent, exaggerated or fabricated a single thing, honest! If you have a hard time believing any of this, then ask another missionary or come over for a visit and see for yourself! It's not just Ukraine that you could visit to find these kinds of things happening. Whenever anyone moves to another culture, it's always different than what you're use to, no matter what country you move to.

I've written about these funny or unusual experiences not to offend the Ukrainian people, but to share how God has allowed me to live cross-culturally without losing my mind! Finding the humor in life is the best way for me to deal with it! I'm sure a Ukrainian, who has moved to America, can write the same kind of book telling about how crazy Americans do this and that and how weird our culture is. We do have a lot of strange things going on in America too. Do we really know why we do the things we do? Not always, it's just a part of our culture, and that's the way **we** do it.

Just because Ukrainians do things a certain way, that I think are bizarre or wrong, doesn't necessarily make it so. I just think this way because of my culture: the way I've been raised by my family and my country. You really are raised by your country too. I never thought about being from a particular culture until I experienced living in one different from my own.

Now I do believe there are some things that one culture may do better or worse than others. We all do lots of things differently that really don't matter, but there are also lots of cultural things all over the world **that are wrong**. They're wrong, because they obviously go against God's word, which applies to all people no matter what country you're in or what your culture has to say about it. Sometimes it's hard to know exactly how to handle a cultural situation according to God's word, but if you seek God's wisdom on it long enough, He'll show you how to handle it. God's word doesn't change, but the application of it can be different in different cultural situations. I think this is one area, of many, that is hard for missionaries living cross-culturally.

At first, I was only going to write about the lighter side of my missionary experience, but since there is too much despair here to always find a humorous escape, I felt compelled to share at least some of the seriousness of our mission. I want you to laugh and enjoy what you read, as well as, gain an understanding of the struggles of life in the former Soviet Union. Even though there has been independence gained, the people here are still looking for a political solution, to fill a void only Christ can fill. I hope you will be amused but also challenged to be a missionary right where you are and be available to God to wherever He may lead you.

INTRODUCTION

How Did We End Up In Ukraine?

In 1979, during our college years, my boy friend and I went to a Christian conference after Christmas. It was during this conference that Timmy and I gave ourselves whole heartedly to the Lord and told him we were available to Him to do whatever, whenever and wherever. We had no idea what the future would hold, but just wanted to let God lead us there. We graduated from Clemson University and in 1982 were married in our hometown of Florence, South Carolina, where we remained and were involved in college ministry at the local university. We were blessed by all the Lord did there, but decided to move back to Clemson in 1984 to be in fellowship with the body of believers we had left when we graduated.

We continued in ministry opportunities, and in 1990 we went into full-time ministry with Great Commission Ministries. We had our third child in 1991 and life was good. We worked mostly with college students and were happy in what we were doing, but God had something new on our horizon.

In the summer of 1996, Timmy was asked to go on a two week mission trip to Ukraine. He'd been thinking about going to Asia on a trip, but I thought he should go with our good friend Steve Nelson, who had wanted him to go to Russia or Ukraine for some time. I gave Timmy my blessings, but said, "Just don't come back saying we're moving there!"

But then it happened, Timmy returned and he was so excited! As he shared with me all he had experienced, I felt in my heart God was doing something. Timmy knew me well, and knew that I would like Ukraine. I realized then that I needed to experience what God was doing in Ukraine for myself, so three months later we went back to Ukraine, so I could check it out. I had never traveled overseas before. I had already asked if Ukraine had any weird animals or giant spiders and they don't, and they do have M&Ms, so I'd be ok!

It was not the best time of year to visit. It was October and for most of the two weeks we were there, it was cold and dreary. It was such a dismal, depressing picture. Amazingly, this didn't seem to bother me. God had been working in my heart before I got there, so this awful, first impression didn't deter my interest. Soon we met with some Ukrainian believers who were really excited that we were scouting out the land and thinking of moving there. I immediately fell in love with them, but later, the unbelievers were the ones who really touched my heart. I was seeing Ukraine through God's eyes.

We went to a boarding house, for children who lived near Chernobyl, whose health had been compromised. We were there doing some activities and ministering to the kids and afterwards the director and about six of her staff, all women, asked us into her office. She then asked us this question: "How did you become Christians, and why should we become Christians." I couldn't believe my ears! I immediately thought to myself, "I'm movin' **here**!" I was already packing in my mind! We were then able to share our testimonies and the Gospel with them. We had other opportunities to share the Gospel as well, so after seeing the interest, and experiencing things like this, how could I not move to Ukraine! God was going to have to give me a good reason **to stay** in America!

I returned home about to burst! I could hardly keep my mouth from blurting out, "We're moving to Ukraine!" (Probably experiencing jet lag for the first time kept me from doing this!) I've always been the type that knows what God wants me to do a little quicker than most people, but Timmy is not so hasty. He likes to wrestle through stuff before anything's official, so I had to hold my tongue! We had to take the proper steps and see what the Lord wanted us to do next. Our church body prayed and fasted about God's will concerning our desire to move to Ukraine.

Our decisions to go ahead with the next steps were confirmed over and over to us. I had some very specific requests of God. I told the Lord, "If you want us to move there, these things need to happen: first, my mother won't have a heart attack when I tell her.

Second, the kids will want to move too, and third, the house needs to sell very quickly, so I won't lose my mind having to keep it clean all the time!"

Well, my mom didn't have a heart attack, and actually held her tongue; two miracles in one! So now the next thing to do was to take our kids to Ukraine and see how they would like it. This was no big deal since they had already, in their short lives, lived away from home during the summers on many mission trips in the states and also for two weeks planting a church in Costa Rica. They were troopers! But this would be more of a real test, not just a quick mission trip. So the summer of 1997 would give us a little taste of what it would be like living there. We hoped our kids: Micah (10), Dawson (8), and Laurel (6) were up for the challenge. I was hoping it wouldn't be a trial period full of trials.

Well, it was a great six weeks, with never a dull moment. I got a good dose of what it's like not just visiting but living in a different culture; the **Ukrainian** culture. And when I say different, I mean **different!** I didn't know I was going to have all these crazy things to write about in a book! It was much more of a challenge than our life in America, but the kids were happy, so we were happy. When our six weeks were up, they were sad that our time was over. They had had a great time, especially with the Ukrainians. They let us know they were willing to make the move. We were **so** blessed by our kid's attitudes. This made all the difference. We would have never moved our kids somewhere they didn't want to go. It had always been important to us for our kids to feel a part of whatever ministry we were involved in, and we wanted this to continue in Ukraine as well.

Now all we needed was for the house to sell. Well, it only took twelve days and without a realtor! My mom was so shocked. She said, "Either God must really want you in Ukraine or you need to stay here and go into real estate!"

I went to Kiev, right after we sold our house, to look for an apartment to rent. I was there a week and God blessed us with a good place in the perfect location. While I was gone, Timmy finished moving everything out of the house. We had already packed up the stuff we were keeping and had given away our furniture. We just had some boxes of junk to sort through, but it was weird coming back; I was homeless.

The people that bought our house had already sold theirs and needed to move as soon as possible into ours, so we closed the deal and moved in with some friends six weeks before we left for Ukraine. This was a difficult six weeks, having to live and finish packing some where else, but we survived.

On June 12, 1998, we left South Carolina and arrived in Kiev, Ukraine the next day. Our fellow missionaries had arranged a bus to carry us and our twenty-three pieces of luggage and boxes to our new home. Boy! Were we a spectacle pulling up to the apartment building! We were all jet lagged, but excited just to be settled. We were so glad to have somewhere to call home; the living in limbo was over.

This was only the beginning of our cross-cultural experience. We didn't know all that was in store for us, but we knew we were in God's will, and there was no safer place in the world to be! Let the adventure begin!

PART I

THE LIGHTER SIDE

CHAPTER 1

LOST IN TRANSLATION

The phrase, "Lost in translation," never really meant that much to me, until I had to live in a land of little English. Now I know this phrase is so very true. My husband speaks Russian very well after years of studying, but still likes to use a translator when he wants to make sure he's clearly communicating something important. He knows enough to understand if they are translating correctly what he is saying, but many times he has stopped and told his interpreter that what he said in English is not what he heard come out of the interpreter's mouth in Russian. For example: when we say something is "exciting," they use the Russian word for "interesting." When we use the word "interesting" in English, it can be positive as in "an interesting documentary" or negative as in "that person has interesting taste in clothes." I've notice in American films that the way they translate certain things is not the same and loses some of its meaning and effectiveness, but only one who knows both languages knows the difference.

I've heard it said that Russian will be the language in Heaven, because it will take an eternity to learn! This is true in my opinion. It is really a difficult language, especially for someone like me who can't memorize worth a toot! First of all, it doesn't help that the Russian language uses the Cyrillic alphabet. This alphabet, interestingly enough, was developed so this part of the world could have the Bible in the same language. That's a good thing. All the countries of The **F**ormer **S**oviet **U**nion all spoke Russian, so this is one reason we've learned Russian instead of Ukrainian. If we were to ever move to another part of the FSU, there would be Russian speakers there, even if they have gone back to their national tongue since independence.

The Cyrillic alphabet has thirty-two letters. There are a few that are the same as ours; yeah!!!! I love these letters and am thankful for them! And then there are the letters that look the same as ours but aren't! I don't like these letters! It took me a while to get over these letters and come to terms with this confusion; like I needed more! Our letter "P" is their letter "R." I first noticed this in the signs that read, "6ap"(BAR), where you can get yourself a drink. Our letter "H" is their letter "N." Our letter "C" is their letter "S." And there are a few more! Do you see what I'm talking about here?

It's funny seeing some words that are suppose to be the same as some English words of ours, which start with the letter "H," but since they don't have the letter "H" sound exactly, they use their letter that is the sound of our letter "G" instead. So when you're at McDonald's, you can order a **g**amburger, you can go on a trip to **G**awaii and stay in a **g**otel, read your **G**arry Potter book and go to the drugstore and get some medicine for your **g**emorrhoids! And don't forget that famous Nazi guy, Adolf **G**itler!

Then there are some confusing words that were formed just to aggravate me! What do you suppose the Russian word for orange juice would be? Well, it's pronounced as if spelled *applesin*. In the first year, many times I'd forget and ask for what I thought was going to be apple juice and got orange! And what fruit would you think a *pearsic* would be? Wrong! It's a peach! I feel like someone did this just to annoy **me**!

There are many words that the Russian language uses that are the same as our words, just pronounced a little different with a Russian accent. Since most people here, that know English, learned British English, some of the English words we do have in common will have a British pronunciation. When I'm in a situation and don't know a Russian word, which is often, when in doubt, I try the English word! This method has saved me quite a bit. Sometimes it's close enough; I'm understood and my mission is accomplished.

Our son's name sounds like another word in Russian. Micah pronounced in English is the same pronunciation as an underwear T- shirt in Russian. When we would call out for Micah in a public place, the Ukrainians must have thought, "What a weird name, poor kid."

One word that is pronounced the same in both languages, but has a different meaning, is the word *preservative*. Just until recently, when they have used this word, they were talking about a type of birth control! So who knows what they're thinking when they hear Americans speaking in English, about not liking additives and preservatives and so forth, and they hear one word they recognize! You'll hear more about this particular preservative, and where you can buy it, later in the book.

There are many Russian words that sound alike, and we sometimes stress the wrong syllable and say something crazy or embarrassing. During the first few years, the only grocery stores were these small little buildings or booths, and you had to ask a clerk for everything. This made it very difficult, for a foreigner like me who didn't speak the language, to get what I needed without making a complete fool of myself; I made "looking like a fool," easy, so I decided to just go with it, and it's worked out pretty well for me.

Once I asked for a bag of flour and apparently my pronunciation was a little off. I know this because she gave me a strange look and repeated the word back to me. I'm thinking, "Isn't that what I said," but apparently not. This look and repeating what I had just said was a common event in my daily life. This time instead of asking for flour, I had mistakenly asked for a bag of **torture**! Little did she know **I was already being tortured** and just wanted a bag of flour!

Well, I finally got home with my bag of flour. It was closed with a row of staples. When I went to open it, one of the staples fell into the bag. Poof! How in the world was I going to find it? I didn't have a sifter. I hated to have to spend too much time looking for it, but I hated to throw out the whole bag of flour, after what I had gone through to get it. I thought if I had a magnet, maybe I could fish it out! I remembered we had a screwdriver that was magnetized at the tip. So I got it, clean the tip, fished one minute and caught me a staple! I'm glad they've quit with those stapled bags now.

Another word that gave me trouble was the word for *one- hundred.* It sounds like the word for *what?* I would find myself repeating my question to a clerk when she had already answered me "One hundred." I thought she was hard of hearing!

I also can get the word for *Jesus* confused with the word for *vinegar.* Now this could be pretty serious when sharing the Gospel! I use vinegar a lot here, but I need Jesus a lot more! Once one of our missionary friends asked some new believers to a Friday night gathering of music, singing and fellowship, but instead used the word for a "drunken party!" No wonder these new friends had puzzled looks on their faces! Have you ever thought about foreigners in America making the same mistakes with their broken English? We have quite a few words that sound alike too. For example: one of our friends jokingly thanked us for our hostility instead of our hospitality.

Another time, one of our pastor friends was yelling for everyone to leave one room and enter another for a time of singing. He thought he was saying in Russian, "Let's go sing," but he was actually saying the equivalent of some very derogatory words for "Let's go pee!" A red faced Ukrainian grabbed a hold of our enthusiastic friend to set him straight!

Once during his Russian lesson, Timmy was telling his tutor about dropping off our children at the neighbor's. She asked "You did what?" He realized then he must have said it wrong. Instead of saying the words for, *dropped off*, he said he had *hung* the children at our neighbor's! Timmy has improved a great deal in speaking Russian over the years. I don't think we've had a single hanging since then!

Some of our friends had gotten two kittens unaware of their medical issues. Well, they had a Ukrainian friend call the vet and make an appointment for them. The Russian word for doctor is *vrach*, but our friends misunderstood and thought this was the doctor's name, so they were calling him Dr. Vrach (Dr. Doctor), until someone finally told them of their blooper!

European time (military time) really makes, more sense than the we tell time in America. For one thing, saying AM and PM are eliminated. It's another part of the language that can be misunderstood by Ukrainians because the Americans don't use it correctly. I rarely use the European way, but try to be more careful and make sure I'm understood. Once, in our early years, we met someone new at church and Timmy wanted to talk more to him, so he asked the guy if they could talk some more by phone the next day. When the man asked, "What time should I call?" Timmy said without thinking, "5:00." Well, sure enough our phone rang at exactly 5:00 AM the next morning! Timmy answered the phone and heard, "How are you doing?" Timmy told him he was sleeping! He asked this man why in the world was he calling so early (well actually, I don't know exactly what Timmy was saying in Russian) and the guy said he was just doing what he had been asked to do, which was to call at 5:00. Then Timmy realized the mistake he had made, but who would think someone wanted to be called that early in the morning? Who wouldn't question that! Once again we were reminded we weren't in SC anymore.

Making mistakes can be costly not only in monetary matters and personal embarrassment, but in making horrible messes of situations. Take getting your hair done, for instance. Would you really want to have your hair done by someone you cannot communicate with because of the language barrier? When I decided I needed a, "new do," while in Budapest during our staff retreat I did exactly that. Not only was I getting my hair done, but I was getting my first international perm! Naturally I was a bit weary when I met the hair dresser, whose hair was hot pink on top and black on the bottom. After overcoming my first impression, I sat in her chair comforted by the radio, which was playing, "I Feel Good," by South Carolina native, James Brown. We then moved on to what I wanted done to my hair that day, translated to the hairdresser in Hungarian. The assistant didn't speak English, but she spoke German, so my missionary friend Lori, from Germany who was with us for the retreat, took my English, translated it into German so the assistant could tell the hairdresser in Hungarian! It wasn't the best perm I had ever had, but considering how the hairdresser looked, I think I came out looking pretty good!

The next year, I was with one of my neighbors and noticed how nice her permed hair looked. I asked her where she got it done, and she told me right across the street from our building. I asked her if she'd make me an appointment with the same woman and go with me get mine done. She agreed and I went in hopes of getting a good looking do! Well, every thing turned out just great. The perm was an Italian product (which I was glad of after having heard stories about Ukrainian ones) and it was the best perm I'd ever had.

When it came time to get another perm, I had my neighbor make me another appointment at the same place. This time I didn't feel like I needed any one to go with me to translate any thing. Well, I was wrong. I got to the salon and there was a different girl working there than before. I was a little concerned about this. She began to roll my hair with these wooden perm rods that looked like something they had borrowed from Wilma Flintstone! She rolled up the first rod, dabbed solution on it and continued to do this. By the time she had one side of my hair rolled, each rod had been cooking my hair for a while. I was pretty worried as I could feel my hair frying on one side, long before she had even rolled the other. My **pretty** worried was about to turn into **ugly** worried! I didn't know whether to try and say something or call Timmy and have me put on the prayer chain! After it was all done, I could have won, "Best of Show," in the poodle division!

Once I went shopping for two bedside tables. One of the Russian words for this type of table is pronounced just like our word *commode*, which I think is used sometimes for this piece of furniture in America too, but not by me. Well anyway, I felt really funny telling my friend Sanich, who was driving me to the store, that I needed a commode for each side our bed; one for Timmy and one for me! How convenient!

Now, I'm not trying to be gross here, but we just saw a Russian sign on the top of this new food stand that serves meat in a pita, but weirdly enough, it kind of goes with the previous story. The sign said in Russian, " дуду денер" which pronounced says, "Doo Doo Dinner!" We laughed and can't imagine what this is supposed to mean in Russian, but doesn't sound too appetizing to us Americans!

We have a friend named Sanich who is my own personal taxi whenever I need a car. He speaks just a little English, so with my little bit of Russian, we have our own way of communication. He knows my life so well because of all my shopping. I could probably just send him to the store with my list, without me. He knows exactly where I want to go and why. We have a great time trying to talk and we enjoy trying to figure out what each other is trying to say.

One day we were at the market, about to get out of the car, when we noticed a guy standing in front of our car who had something wrong with his ear. It looked like he had half an ear! We hadn't said a word yet, and when we turned and looked at each other, we both said, exactly at the same time, "Mike Tyson!" We laughed, not believing that we were both thinking the same thing. We do speak the same language after all! Who would have ever thought that the name Mike Tyson would be part of a funny memory of a missionary!

We love to see how things are translated in English on some of the restaurant menus. The Chinese restaurants are the best and most entertaining. They go from Chinese to Russian then to English. I think this is how the unusual translation is created. They call the restaurant's seating capacity the number of "landing spots," and the way they describe the chef preparing the food sounds as if the chef is the one being cooked and prepared! Even in the bathroom there is a translation blooper. The sign reads, "Please **flash** the toilet!" Don't they realize every one flashes the toilet, they just don't all flush?

One thing that has been entertaining is the translations of American movie titles. It's like they watch it first, then they decide what they want to call it. They hardly ever just translate it exactly the same as the American title. For example: The James Bond movie "Die Another Day," is written, "Die, But Not Right Now." "We are Marshall," is written, "We are One Team," and "The Heartbreak Kid," was translated, The Girl That is My Terror." Sometimes, we have to look at the pictures on the video box or DVD to see if we can tell if it's the movie we're looking for.

I've made some other observations that have let me know I'm not the only one that doesn't know all that's being said or written. Some of the Ukrainians are in the dark too! I can't imagine buying a shirt that has words written on it that I can't read. Here, I've had a few laughs when I've seen people who have done this. A Ukrainian pastor's wife, who was pregnant at the time, was wearing a top that had the letters D & G on the front, which are the initials for a big European fashion company. This was not really one of their shirts. Well, underneath the letters it read, "Drunk and Gorgeous;" this is **not** what the letters stand for. When we asked her if she knew what her shirt said, of course she said no, so we told her. She laughed along with us, but was shocked at what she was wearing. On another occasion, I saw a woman with a shirt on that said, "Black History Month." Believe me, they've never celebrated this in Ukraine, and she had no idea what she was wearing.

Since there are a lot of second hand clothing stores and markets here, you can find many things from America. I love to see an old Babushka wearing a sweater advertising some golf resort, or NFL team. If they like it, it doesn't matter what it says. They most likely won't come in contact with anyone that can read it any way.

Also many times there is American music playing in the stores. The store manager and most of the people shopping, don't understand the songs. I was very offended while shopping one day when a store had music just blaring; it was a very graphic rap song full of foul language. We've asked McDonalds to turn off offensive music before, as well as asking taxi drivers to change radio stations.

It's rare that you hear someone speaking English in a store or out on the streets, so I was very surprised to hear a Ukrainian man calling out an American man's name outside of our apartment building one day. This man was yelling. "Bill! Bill!" I thought he must have an American friend visiting or maybe there was another American man living in our neighborhood that I didn't know about. Well, it wasn't long before Bill came running up to the guy. Bill was his dog!

After hearing and seeing another person call their dog Linda and another one Bob, I realized that a lot of Ukrainians use American names for their dogs. I'm not so sure how we're supposed to take this; I guess it's a compliment. I just wish you could **hear** them calling their dogs. You'd really get a kick out of hearing these names being called out with their accent, "Leenda, Leenda!"

I never heard anyone use an American name to call a cat, because everyone knows you don't call cats by name when you want them. I kind of thought everyone in the world said, "Here kitty, kitty, kitty," but they don't! Out of habit I tried to use the American cat call, but it didn't even get a glance from a stray cat, much less get one to run towards me. Then someone told how it works in Ukraine. You make a sound as if you're saying kiss, kiss, kiss real fast. Works every time!

My daughter, who was six years old at the time, realized right away that everyone didn't speak or understand English. She was trying to get rid of a pesky fly that was buzzing around her, so she said the all American, "Shoo, fly, shoo!" Then I heard her say,

"Oh! That fly doesn't know what I'm saying, he doesn't understand English!"

Sometimes people in our building, or on public transportation, will make a comment about us, thinking we don't understand Russian, but Timmy knows what they're saying. Once he was taking out our trash, which is always a huge garbage bag, and someone coming in the building said in Russian, "Can you believe those Americans make that much garbage?" It is embarrassing having more garbage than anyone else in our building and worse is seeing people going through it in the dumpster.

Since living in Ukraine, the Lord has made me much more aware of how a foreigner must feel when they are in America. Even though I was involved with ministering to some international students while I was living in a college town, I wish now that I had made much more of an effort to help them in any way that I could have. Now that I have been in their shoes, I see how Christians living in America could have such a great opportunity to minister to the aliens in their midst. It would be great if believers and others would see these people as God sees them, not just as legal or illegal.

We have realized it is difficult sometimes to express yourself in another language, especially when sharing things that have made you who you are. At these moments it's not only the language barrier but also the cultural differences. Your culture has formed you and your language is the biggest part of that, so some things just don't translate. Aren't you glad God knows all our languages; our thoughts that we can't even express. He sees into the deepest parts of our heart and nothing is ever lost in translation with Him.

CHAPTER 2

EUROPEAN

(You're apeein' alright!)

It didn't take long for me to realize that our cultures were also different in the way people chose to relieve themselves. I've never been too fond of public bathrooms, even in America, but living in Ukraine took "public" to a whole new level! After visiting my first public bathroom, I could hardly blame people for using the bathroom outside. I'll tell you more about this use of the great outdoors later.

Here they just use the word toilet; they don't use other words like restroom or bathroom. Have you ever wondered why we use these words? Well, I hurriedly entered into the subway restroom and I'm not talking about the place you get sandwiches! Here I go, unaware, not being forewarned by anyone! Had this been done to me on purpose? I paid thirty kopecks, which was about six cents. With this payment came an eight inch piece of toilet paper and Charmin it wasn't! When we first moved here, the only kind of toilet paper they had was this rough, "paper bag brown" colored stuff that came from a holeless roll. My mother had told me about this paper after visiting Russia in the seventies. She said, "Now I know why they drink vodka- so they can use the toilet paper!"

After receiving my little strip of unattractive, never been tried out by the inventor TP, I headed for a stall. There were quite a few stalls in this concrete, dimly lit, smelly place. Smelly doesn't quite describe it, you had to be there! Before turning in, I couldn't help but notice all these women's heads above the stalls. I wondered, "What in the world was going on in here?" I entered the stall and there was no toilet! I couldn't believe I had picked a stall without a toilet. What I did see was a platform which consisted of two flat, iron looking spots where you put your feet and a hole in the middle. Judging by the other ladies stances, I figured out what to do. If only I had been warned, I could have practiced the "squatty potty" technique before attempting such a feat, but I think you have to be born in Ukraine to know how to really use these things. Later, I saw variations of these toilets that were ceramic things on the floor that looked like toilets that had run over by a steam roller. The same technique was required.

It wasn't long before I realized that "you get what you pay for!" I was so traumatized during my first public bathroom experience; I didn't even get to go! I ran out of there so fast, I probably had some brown toilet paper stuck to the heel of my shoe. I just wanted some fresh air before I lost my lunch. I didn't care about getting my six cents worth; I could hold it! ·

Some other europeen'moments include: those who have had the misfortune of dropping their cell phones down the hole and worse, retrieving them! One of our friends did get his out, but only to get teased about having a "crappy" connection. He tried to have it repaired, but it was totaled. Even if he had gotten it to work, it would have been a hassle having to hook an air freshener to it!

Even ten years later, they still have these squatty potties. I noticed one of our department stores had brand new ones. The best toilets are in the nice restaurants, like McDonalds. When this American icon first opened here, its bathrooms were sparkling clean for the first minute only. When I went in, I couldn't believe that the toilet seats were almost black from people's shoes. They stood on the seats as if they were standing over the ceramic holes in the ground! I was shocked, but this was what they were used to. Years later at some of the McDonald's, to keep out those just looking for a bathroom, you have to have your receipt which has a code for opening the bathroom door.

I also noticed that when there was an actual toilet in other public buildings, there was never a toilet seat on it. Once we had a conference in an old, but fairly nice auditorium in the center of Kiev and a Ukrainian working with our mission, who was in charge of things, brought in toilet seats just for the conference, and took them off after our meeting was done. Does she have a special closet in her apartment where she keeps used toilet seats?

Whenever we would see a puddle in our apartment building elevator, I immediately warned the kids that this was no ordinary puddle! Now I know you're thinking "No way, gross…"but yes, it's true. People will just come in off the street and use your building's elevator as a toilet. I've even seen worse in the stairwells! Now a lot of apartment buildings have entrance doors that can only be opened with a code. Many apartments have residents who take shifts as hired guards to keep out those who would do such things and others that have no business in our building. I've also noticed some stickers in some elevators that say, "This is not a toilet."

Now let me tell you about those poor souls who just can't hold it any longer, not able to find a public toilet, or get to an elevator. They become very public by choosing various outside spots along their way. You can especially smell where people have been when you're cutting between or behind a building. The metro stations really reek in the mornings after people have come through there late at night and couldn't, or wouldn't, hold it.

Once we lived in an apartment, on the sixth floor, conveniently across from the dumpsters. Between these dumpsters and a small utilities building, was a much frequented bathroom stop. People thought since they had something blocking them on the sides that they weren't being seen, but they weren't blocked on my side! Many a time I wanted to yell out the window and ask "Feel better now?!" It would mostly be men making a quick stop, but I did see women too. There's nothing like a full moon during the middle of the day to remind you of why you need to get those mini-blinds up!

Its one thing to see it from my apartment window, but to have someone just a foot away relieving himself is another. I was waiting to get on a tram, and a man was going right beside me! He seemed drunk and when a drunk's got to go, he's got to go! I'm used to seeing people going in corners, beside trees and other places, but this was a little too close to my personal space!

Many times throughout the day I've see people using the bathroom outside. Many are little babies and children. They are assisted by their parents near a bush, alley way, or just off to the side of the sidewalk. Sometimes they don't wear underwear or a diaper so they can go more quickly and easily. I'm not as bothered by the little ones as I am with the full grown goers. Sometimes you see someone pointing or squatting behind a tree, but they forget that the people driving down the street on the other side of the tree are getting a full view.

Just when I thought I had seen or heard it all, a friend of mine witnessed someone with a real bladder control issue! They couldn't believe their ears, they heard it first. It was the trickling sound of a small brook or water fall. They were on an escalator in the subway station, and two men further up were letting it go, and down it flowed, trickling over the moving stairs!

Then there is the groups of europeen' guys at the soccer games. They are full of beer, and whatever, standing on top of an embankment, relieving themselves throughout the game! It runs down the hill as the grossest little river you've ever seen! My husband and sons have told me about this. All the more reason for me **not** to become a soccer fan!

I don't think I ever thanked the Lord a single time for any public bathroom in America, but now I know better. So the next time you're in a disgusting, gas station bathroom, remember there are worse places to have to go!

CHAPTER 3

TRANSPORTATION: EVERY MAN FOR HIMSELF

Transportation is different in every culture. In Ukraine it's not only different but down right crazy! Let's start with cars. I've never experienced anything like it in America because if Americans drove like they do in Ukraine, they'd all be in jail and being the sane driver that I am, I'd have the road to myself! I think they have some rules of the road, but as far as I can tell, people just take them as suggestions or not at all. The traffic has become unbearable the last couple of years. The former communist government just didn't plan on people progressing in their lives, having cars and such, so the city doesn't have the capacity to handle the traffic. I've read since October, 2007, an average of fifty thousand newly registered cars hit the streets of Kiev every month. This leaves too many cars with no place to go.

Since we don't have a car here, we have to use taxis and other public transportation. The risk is great, but sometimes you have to take the risk. When I first moved here, it took some getting use to one of the best ways to get where you're going- hitch-hiking! It's like going back in time in America, when it was a great way to get around, and you didn't fear for your life as the driver or the passenger. Here, you just stick out your hand, and a car will stop fairly quickly; usually it's just one man. You tell him where you need to go and then agree on a price. This was always a cheap way to go before gas prices went sky high. You never quite know what they'll want to charge, but we usually have a price in mind and try to stick with it. One day Timmy and I got a taxi to a place for $6, and when we were ready to go home, we came out and asked another taxi, that was sitting on the corner and he wanted $20 for what we had just paid $6 for! We told him to forget it! Sometimes they think we're tourist and that we don't know what we should be paying.

Are We There Yet?

I can't begin to count how many times I've stuck my hand out and been picked up by a man I've never met. Every car is a potential taxi. The car doesn't have to say *taxi* on it. In all my years here, I've only been picked up once by a woman driver. There aren't as many women drivers over all, but a lot more now than years ago. I lived here four months before seeing my first woman driver. For Ukrainians to even get a license here is an enormous hassle. They usually won't pass you the first couple of times, so most people bribe the instructors; they know that's what the instructor is waiting for. Now that I think of it, most of the drivers here must have bribed their way to a license long before taking lessons!

I don't mind hitching rides with random strangers, I'm use to it, but I don't like drunken strangers. Alcoholism is one the biggest problems here, so there are probably a good many drunk drivers on the road throughout the day. Amazingly enough, I've only had a few, that have had a few too many! One afternoon we needed to get our daughter to a school event, so we went on the street corner to get a taxi or wave down a random car. Well, there was a taxi driver sitting there in his rundown, red Mercedes. We went through the usual routine and then got in. The three of us were on our way when we notice the bottle of liquor between the two front seats. It didn't take us long to realize this swerving driver was under the influence; besides he was smiling too much for a Ukrainian! We knew it was time to get out when the guy picked up the bottle an offered Timmy a drink! Timmy asked him to pull over immediately and let us out. We had planned to pick up a friend who was already waiting for us a couple blocks away, so we stopped right in front of her and got out.

Since we had to bail out of the first taxi, Timmy stuck out his hand and flagged down another man to take us. We were already about thirty minutes in to our trip across town when we realized we had passed the street we should have turned on. We asked the driver about it, and he said he needed to find a gas station. At the time, this was a hard thing to do because there was a problem with the gasoline trade with Russia, and our supply had been interrupted during this particular week. There weren't many stations open due to the lack of fuel. Well sure enough, we ran out of gas before we found a station. After paying the driver a portion of the original agreement, the four of us got out to flag another driver down. At this point, we were already late to the event in which our daughter was a part of. It had never taken us more than one taxi to get to this destination before, and who knew just how many it was going to takes us this time; we still weren't there!

A car pulls over; we go through the rig- a -ma -roll once again. I wondered if this guy was up for the challenge and could complete the journey! We're off, riding along and suddenly he turns down a side street that is not a direct route to where we need to go. We asked him about his choice of the scenic route, and he said he wanted to get off the main road to avoid the police, because he didn't have any documents; meaning no license, registration, etc. Well, he finally got us there. We couldn't believe it when we reached our destination. A twenty to thirty minute trip had turned into more than an hour long fiasco!

Many times I'll flag down a car, get in and put on my seatbelt, which happens to be the law. The next thing I know, the driver is going on an on about how I don't need to put it on, how he's a safe driver. They take it as an insult, but nonetheless, no matter how good a driver he is, I still have to worry about all the other crazy people zooming in and out on all sides!

Let Me out of This Car!

I think Ukrainians pride themselves in creative ways to get through traffic. If it's a three lane road, then it's good for at least five or six cars across. Oh, and don't forget the sidewalk, it's always considered an extra lane when there is a traffic jam or when you're just wanting to beat everyone else there! This can be quite annoying, not to mention dangerous, if you're walking down the sidewalk. When drivers do this, it backs up traffic because you eventually have to let these sidewalk maniacs back into the flow of traffic when the sidewalk comes to an end. It's not just cars that use the side walks; you can get hit by a truck or bus too! They haven't realized that if everyone obeyed the rules, then things would move much more smoothly, quickly and safely.

The absolute craziest stunt that I've experienced, more than once mind you, is the decision to make your own lane, in on coming traffic! Yes, I'm telling the truth! When in a traffic jam, someone will choose to go into oncoming traffic, just slide right over into the oncoming lane or even cross over a grass median or ditch to get there! If you try to say something or **scream** while peeping through your hand covered face, they just look at you and say "Normalna," which means "this is normal." I just want to say "NOT where I come from!" Just recently I noticed that they put up a barrier to divide a major highway that has eight lanes across. It's known for a lot of accidents, but hopefully this will help.

Who Needs a Gas Station?

Our friend Robbie said he once hitched a ride out on the highway and after a little while the guy suddenly stopped out in the street. They had run out of gas. Robbie didn't know what the man had in mind when he saw him trying to flag down different cars. A car stopped and the other driver began to siphon gas from his car into the empty one, right out in the middle of a busy highway! When he had enough gas, the guy paid this newly hired gas attendant for his services. How convenient; he didn't have to bother with getting his car out of the road, getting a ride to the gas station and then getting back to fill his car up.

The Marshrutka.

Besides all the taxis, we have all sorts of public transportation in Kiev. It's very organized, and you can get anywhere in or out of town. There are electric trolley buses, that run on electric lines above them and trams that are also electric, but run on a track. Then there are regular buses of all shapes and sizes, and some over-sized vans that are called *marshrutkas*.

Once I had bought a birthday present for one of my sons and attempted to bring it home on a marshrutka van. It was a small, plastic aquarium with fake fish that bobbled around in water. The fish might not have been real, but the water sure was! I didn't think about emptying it; it looked tightly sealed and was in a box, but sure enough the water started to slosh around and leak onto the floor. It was getting dark and I hoped no one would notice the stream of water starting to run down the floor of the van. My pants were also getting wet, and I was sure someone was going to think I had had a little, "accident." I was so glad when my stop came, and I could get off and get home.

I've been on buses with a few groceries, trying my hardest to keep my stuff from getting smashed. Once I barely fit inside the bus, and the door closed on me and my eggs! Since I didn't know how to say, "I'm stuck in the door!" in Russian, I let out some kind of yelp, which must have been an international distress call. He opened the door again, but then it closed on my foot. By the time I got home and got supper on the table, I dared anyone not to eat what was put in front of them!

Another time, I had to take a cake to a PTA meeting. It cost a lot to go by taxi, so I went by bus. The bus was packed, I didn't get a seat, and I had to hold this covered 9x13 cake pan vertically most of the way! I was getting concerned that the icing was going to start oozing out of the pan at any moment, since I had iced it when it was still a little warm. I was picturing it running off the cake, out of the pan and on to the crowd! Thankfully another woman, who was seated near where I was standing, offered to hold it for me. I was glad to get off that bus and be able to check on the cake. Well, let's say it tasted better than it looked!

Watch Your Pockets!

When you're crammed in with the public like this, you have to watch out for pick pockets. When you've got people pressed in against you and haven't put your valuables in out of reach places, it's hard to know if someone's making off with something like your wallet or cell phone. I've even heard of people having their coat pockets sliced open with some kind of blade, by a thief who's trying to steal their valuables. Once I was standing in a full tram with a Ukrainian friend, and she spoke firmly to a guy that was standing next to me. She had spoken Russian, so I was curious to what she had said. When we got off, I asked her what that was all about. She said the guy was just about to put his hand in my coat pocket and she said to him, "Don't even think about it!"

Another Ukrainian girl friend of mine had some money stolen from her on the tram. She knew the guy had done it, so when he got off, she got off right behind him, and grabbed her money back. She began to ask him, along with some of his friends who were standing there, about his life of crime, and then started sharing Christ with him as he walked home. She didn't stop there. She went with him inside his home and shared with some of his family members too!

Getting Around Underground

I think the safest and quickest way to get around Kiev is on the subway. They call it the Metro. We have three lines that can get you across the city quickly, and it sure beats sitting in traffic. I like knowing exactly how long a journey will take instead of wondering if I'll ever get there when stuck in traffic that's crawling at a snail's pace.

Late at night, especially on the weekends, it's a little more interesting riding the metro. There's nothing like sitting next to a drunk, sometimes on both sides, and have him keep nodding off, touching your shoulder with his head! I've been the middle of a drunk sandwich on several occasions. If you have a problem with needing your "personal space," don't move here! The metro and all the other public transportation choices will either break you of this issue or send you over the edge! Whatever you're riding is **not** full until you're in pain, and even then, there's always room for one more; at least that's what the people think that are ramming, stuffing and combating their way in!

During rush hour it can get pretty scary if you're claustrophobic. There are points where you're in a sea of people who are coming and going resembling a massive herd of cattle being lead to another location. Well, they're not being led, they're own their own, each cow looking out for their own hide! The crowds bottleneck where you get on the escalator, and this slows the herd down a bit.

Once a friend of mine was taking the metro home after a soccer game, which is especially crowded and her scarf got hung up in the crowd. It was wrapped around her neck and it was being pulled tighter and tighter. She was so packed in bodies; she couldn't even get her hands to her neck to loosen the noose that was choking her. Before it was too late, she was helped by someone and could get her breath again.

On a funnier note, another friend was coming out of a crowded metro car as people were rushing in. Her scarf got hung on a woman who was hurriedly making her way into the car as my friend was exiting. Trying to get unhooked, she quickly jerked her scarf as the metro car was closing and leaving. She got free before being pulled away by her neck, but saw the other lady's zipper of her purse come flying off. At least it was from a purse and not from this lady's clothes. She could have felt a draft or had trouble keeping her skirt up the rest of the day!

All kinds of things can happen when you're in a hurry getting on and off the subway. You have to be careful. I've slipped and fallen on the stairs, fortunately not during rush hour and once I dropped my purse. Normally dropping your purse isn't a big deal, you just pick it back up. But I couldn't just do that, I dropped it on the subway tracks! I had ran down the last few steps to the platform where the train stops. I was trying to catch it before the door closed, but I didn't make it. I thought I felt something slide down my arm, but wasn't sure; I had on a coat. I'm didn't think anything had fallen, because there was just a few inches between the subway car and me. Well, when the train pulled away, there was my purse down below on the subway tracks!

It's about a four foot drop from where I was to the tracks below. My purse wasn't right on the rail, thank goodness, and it hadn't opened. I was so glad my phone, wallet, and all my other junk wasn't splattered all over the track. I wasn't sure what to do. There were a few other women standing there. They motioned as if they would keep an eye on it, while I went to back up the small flight of stairs to the turnstiles where there were some workers. In my own unique, Russian language way, I told them that my bag was down in the tracks. The immediately jumped up and brought this long, wooden pole that had a claw looking tip. Hey, apparently I wasn't the first one that had done something like this! I was relieved to get my purse back, and that I didn't get scolded by the metro worker. I was used to looking foolish, or having something weird happen, so it was just another normal day I guess. Once you're safely on, and crammed in, you can also do some shopping. There are usually people selling small items such as: toothbrushes and paste, sewing kits, maps, magazines, and the most popular of all, band aids. It seems like each time the metro stops, another bandage sales person gets on. In addition to venders there are also singers and musicians who come strolling through, so you can give your money to them. They conveniently hang a bag at the end of their accordion or guitar for you to drop money into. Most of the time it's pleasant, but sometimes I've wanted to give them money **not** to sing!

In the winter it's not so bad to have a zillion bodies keeping you warm, but in the summer, you're plenty warm, so it's another sense that gets activated. When on a packed metro, you can hold on to some handles or a bar just above your head. When you're crammed in and have nowhere to go, you might as well come to terms with the armpits that are up in the air right in your face. A drunk sandwich or armpit sandwich? Tough call! They both have their own unique aroma.

Winter has its drawbacks too. If you're riding a bus or tram during really cold weather, it's hard sometimes to see where to get off. I've had to scrape ice off the inside of the window to see if I'm at my stop. Birr, that's cold!

The public is welcomed to have their pets on any of the transportation too. I've sat next to many cats and dogs before, fortunately not at the same time. Once we were coming back on a tram from a popular park where people love to walk their dogs. Timmy had about four dogs around his feet, and we're not talking cute little toy poodles! A lot of people here have ferocious looking Rottweilers and Dobermans. There were a few growls of conversation during the ride; Timmy was glad to get to our stop.

Transportation and Confrontation

Sometimes you buy your tram ticket from a ticket lady. I've never understood why they can nab you on the tram for not having a ticket, when you haven't had a chance to buy one yet, but they will.

They'll have two or three bouncers on there, so they can pull you off the tram to confront you about this and make you pay a fine. Once there was only one bouncer, and he attempted to pull an offender off, but had trouble since it was one on one.

They would wrestle each other every time the tram's door would open at a stop, but the bouncer couldn't get him off. I was sitting right near this confrontation, but was used to seeing this sort of thing. What I wasn't used to was one of the tram conductors tearing into the bouncer with a crowbar during one of the wrestling matches! At one of the stops, the conductor was so mad about having to wait on the confrontation at each stop; he went after the bouncer instead of the guy who refused to buy a ticket! He hit him a few times and the bouncer left the tram, and we continued on our route.

I've witnessed many fights on transportation. The most interesting exhibitions are women who get into a brawl. I've seen young and old duke it out while riding or waiting. One day, I observed two women fighting, maybe over the young man who was with them. They were slinging purses and fists and screaming at each other. The most exciting clashes are when two babushkas go at it. You want to stay clear of these, but sometimes you get caught right in the middle of them on public transportation. They are usually just verbal, but I've seen them get physical too! You don't want to get involved with a Babushka that's wound too tight!

When riding any kind of public transportation, you are always supposed to give up your seat for a babushka, when there aren't any seats left. If you don't, you'll usually get an ear full. Most of the time, the men give up their seats for these ladies, because they don't want to risk the tongue lashing they'll get if they don't. But sometimes there are still some men who won't be gentlemen, so some of us younger women will give up our seats instead.

Just the other day, Timmy said he was on the metro and a guy was asked by a babushka for his seat. He wouldn't give it to her! He said he had just as much right to sit there as she did. Boy! Did he say the wrong thing! Timmy said several other people got involved in this one and it heated up! After all was said and done, he still didn't give it up his seat.

Getting to School

Over the years, we've had several ways our children have gotten to school. We've had the blessing of having a school for missionary kids, but it was a challenge getting them there sometimes. They rode a bus for a couple of years with a bunch of their classmates that lived on our side of town. They were the last ones on and the first ones off, so it was a good situation while it lasted. Theses buses weren't your yellow school bus type, but old city buses that had routes throughout the city during the day. The school arranged a deal with two guys to be our school bus drivers, one bus for each of the two sides of town.

Well, one day these guys came into the school office around noon and said, "We can't work for you any more, starting right now; we can't even take the kids home today. Apparently they were about to be caught using these buses as a personal business on the side, and they didn't have permission to. They then said, "You never knew us; we were never here!" Then they walked out. Boy! We sure did appreciate the notice! We were in a pickle, with no transportation at the end of the school day. That was a long time ago and I can't remember what we did that day, but we made temporary arrangements for the next few days with some other bus drivers. When my kids got home after school the next day, I couldn't believe my eyes! They had soot smeared all over their faces; they looked like chimney sweeps! I asked them what in the world happen to them, and they said the old buses they rode home on were terrible and that smoke was billowing up inside the bus! I knew then that the school had to make some other arrangements quickly, because any more days of this would take years off our kid's lives! Thankfully, we soon had better buses.

The next year, we didn't have a bus available, so we went in together with some other families and hired a driver with his personal car to take our kids to school. We were fortunate enough to find a safe and dependable driver by the name of Sanich, who I briefly mentioned earlier. Timmy had met him when flagging down a ride, and he's been driving for us regularly now for years. Getting our kids to school became pretty uneventful, for the most part, but there were some interesting trips once in a while. I remember the day they had a flat tire on the way to school and on the way home too! How can someone have two flat tires in one day? Then there was always the bridge crossing. If they made it across in decent time, they would get to school on time, but you never knew what the traffic was going to be like. One morning, a dog was on the bridge and caused a five car pile up! Well, they were tardy of course, but at least they weren't in the wreck!

I've always hated, and still do hate, having to cross that bridge. The highway has four lanes on both sides, and more if you count the sidewalks! Once it was a half day at school and the teachers were having a work day for the latter half. I decided to take the staff lunch. I carried lasagna enough for thirty or so teachers and was planning on having it there around 12:15. Well, Sanich and I didn't even get to the bridge before the traffic stopped. There had been a wreck, so we were told to turn around. We had to cross at another bridge across town, which meant back tracking, and passing my apartment to get there. With all these extra people having to go to this other bridge, added to the already full highway of the people that normally use this bridge, we had a big mess. I ended up getting the **cold** lasagna there close to 2:00! It was just another day in frustrating traffic. That was in 2005. Now the traffic is a whole lot worse.

Traveling in Ukraine and Beyond

We hardly ever travel by car when we need to go to another city in Ukraine. We usually take a train if it's far away and some other form of public transportation if it's not too far from Kiev. Traveling outside of Kiev is always interesting. You never know what you're in for, especially if you have to cross the border into a neighboring country. One day, Timmy was traveling by bus to another city. Suddenly the engine caught fire and the bus began to fill with smoke. The bus stopped and the driver ordered everyone off. There was no, "Triple A," rushing to their aid; there was no one doing anything. There were no apologies, no instructions or suggestions. Timmy realized it was up to each passenger to find their own way to his or her final destination.

On another trip to a city just across the Russian border, Timmy and our friends, Eric and Cindy, had the usual pain in the neck, "American at the Russian border," experience.

They were running late and missed their bus that would take them across the border, so they flagged down a van that was headed that way. They agreed on a price for their ride and got in. Now they were on their way to Russia with a Russian family. When they got to the border, they were asked to get out of the car, so their passports and visas could be checked. This should only be about a fifteen minute process. This is the time you dread as an American. You're wondering, "What kind of problem will they come up with this time to make you pay a bribe?" Well, of course they "found," something. They told Timmy and his companions that the stamp on their Russian visa was forged! Timmy asked them how could this be, when they had just gotten this stamp on their visa **at** the Russian embassy two days before? After two and a half hours of what felt like KGB interrogation, they finally let them go. And the worst thing of all, the family they hitched a ride with was still waiting for them all that time! They kept thinking it was going to take just a little longer, but it turned into **a lot** longer; it was 2 am.!

Well, if you think they came back a few days later, across the border to Ukraine without any problems, think again. This time they traveled across the border by marshrutka with about fifteen Ukrainians and Russians. This time they said their three year Ukrainian visas weren't valid because there was no such thing as a three year visa!

Timmy asked them, "Well, how have we been allowed in and out of the country so many times at the airport if our visas weren't real?" After forty-five minutes of studying their, "not up to date," rule book, they finally let them pass. Meantime, all the other passengers had been waiting for **THE Americans** to finally be released. Timmy said they were getting some dirty looks and he could hear people talking about them under their breath as they got back on.

Wait, this story isn't finished yet. If you lived here, then you'd know more was bound to happen. And it did! The marshrutka driver was so upset that he was behind schedule; he drove like a madman to make up for the lost time. It wasn't long before this machine he was driving couldn't take the pressure anymore and it blew. The engine was smoking and it was out for the season. They all had to get out, and wave down another ride. They hurriedly squeezed on to an already sardine packed bus, in hope of making their connecting bus back to Kiev. Believe it or not, they made it!

In spring of 2008, we went to Crimea, which is the in the most southern part of Ukraine, on the Black Sea. We went on an overnight train with another couple. It was a seventeen hour trip. When Timmy went to buy our tickets, they didn't have any more compartments left for four people; we could only get two compartments beside each other. We had the top bunks in both rooms. We had no idea who had the lower bunks! This is normal for Ukrainians but not for me! I didn't want to spend the night in a tiny train compartment with two strangers! Timmy had done this before, but without me.

Before we left, we prayed that whoever had the lower bunks would be willing to switch compartments so we could be together with our friends. We figured if it's two young people, they won't mind switching to upper bunks in one of our rooms, if we **pay** them. But if it's two babushkas or dedushkas (grandpas), then we may run into a problem.

We got to the train station, found our train and then our compartments. We were curious to see who were going to be our roommates. Well, it didn't look good when we realized a man and his small child were coming toward us and stopped at our room. There was no way they could switch to another compartment to upper bunks. I thought, "Great! We're going to be cooped up with a kid all night, forget sleeping!" Now we had to wait to see who the next two passengers in the other compartment were going to be. I was asking the Lord to **please** let it be someone who'd be willing to switch.

A young couple got on and came to our second room. We explained the situation and at first they were hesitant, but decided to grant us our request. We offered to pay them, and they took it after we insisted. Our problem was solved. We gave thanks to the Lord for letting us share our tiny room with friends.

We've heard that Ukraine has purchased some nice, new trains, but have yet to travel on one. I've never slept well on a Ukrainian train before, and this trip was no exception. As a matter of fact, it was the worse one yet. I felt like I was trying to sleep through an earthquake! It made so much noise and shook so badly, I knew for sure the engineer had left the tracks and was making his on way through the woods trying to save some time or something! I was miserable. I tossed and turned all night, and if you tossed too much, you could have ended up on the floor from the upper bunk, because they were so narrow.

Not only was it a rough ride, it was a hot ride! They have this thing about drafts, so they won't let you open a window, especially since it wasn't summer yet. It finally cooled off during the night, so **some** people in our compartment were able to sleep. Meanwhile, I stayed awake and tried not to be thrown from my bunk!

I made sure I didn't drink too much before going to the upper deck to sleep. I didn't want to have to climb down to go to the bathroom during the night. It was scary enough during the day to visit this part of the train, and I didn't want to have to attempt such a feat while being out of it during the night. The toilet is pretty gross. I remember seeing a little plaque in an American bathroom that read, "We aim to please, so please aim!" You can imagine how some may miss the mark while trying to stand during such a bumpy ride, which leaves us women with a messy, smelly, situation.

When you flush, it opens up and drops right there on the tracks that you see quickly passing by. I guess this is why they won't let you use the toilet when the train is stopped. Can you imagine what the tracks would look like, and worse, smell like if they did? Train travel is a cheap way to go in the former Soviet Union, but remember, when you have to go, you better have your own roll just in case!

The Changing of the ~~Guards~~ Wheels

At least on my last train trip we didn't have to cross any borders. The communists were really clever back then and fixed it so they couldn't be invaded by rail. They made their tracks a different size than the rest of Europe! So now when you're traveling to another bordering country, they have to stop at the border and change the wheels! There is no way they are going to change their tracks in Ukraine so you have to sit there and wait at the border for the wheels to be changed to the size that fits Poland and everyone else!

I don't know why people can't just get off at the border and take a Polish train to finish their journey. But noooo, that's too easy!

They jack up the train very slowly and quietly then switch the wheels. You don't even have to get off. This is nice, especially since you may cross a border during the night while you're trying to sleep. I learned which train compartment **not** to be in during one of these late night crossing. If you're in the front compartment of the car, they have to come in to your car, go through the floor to turn or unscrew something that's under the train. So if you don't want some men coming in during the night, don't get this compartment.

After the changing of the wheels is finished, you're lowered back down and you're own your way; over two hours later! But wait, don't go back to sleep! Polish customs agents will be making their way to your room in as soon as you're across. They will politely shine a flashlight **in your face**, and your sleeping children's faces, and then check and stamp your passport. Now you may go back to sleep. Sweet dreams.

CHAPTER 4

COMMUNISM: ONE SIZE FITS ALL

With a name like *Kenyon,* I was already used to hearing, "What a unique name," from my fellow Americans. I've been called all kinds of names, even several African countries! Someone in America even addressed a card to me using the name **India**! I guess they couldn't remember my name but knew it sounded like a country. Sorry, wrong continent!

People here have a hard time with my name too; they don't know quite how to say it, plus they don't have all the letter sounds in their alphabet to spell it! I tell them, "Don't worry about it, it's an unusual name in America too.

Anyway, I've been told when you had a child during the days of communism there was a list from which you **had** to choose your baby's name. I don't think there were that many names on the list either. In America we have books of baby names too, but their not published by the government!

It seems like every other guy here is named Sasha! Whenever I'm in doubt of a guy's name, I try Sasha. I have a pretty good chance of being right! It can be a girl's name too. There have been times when we've had four of five Sashas in our house at once. And if it's not Sasha, then it might rhyme with Sasha, like: Masha, Pasha, or Dasha. Some of our friends have come up with other names not on the list since independence; they know they have the freedom to pick something else. It doesn't have to be from the book any more! Still others toil over a week, after the baby's birth, trying to decide what to name their little one, and then they come up with -Sasha! I want to scream, "Come on! You're free, risk it all, go for something new!"

I've always wanted to go to the train station or some where else that's really crowded and yell out, "Saaashhhaaa!" Just to see how many people say, "What?" I'd hate to know I had to pick up someone

I hadn't met yet, named Sasha, from the train station with the only description of, "I'll be wearing black." Do you know how many men I'd be bringing home that fit that description? Several bus loads! People wear a lot of black here. When I first moved I thought, "Where's the funeral?" Or is Johnny Cash playing in town?

We have so many friends with the same first name, it's hard to distinguish who's who, because most of their last names are too hard for me to remember or memorize. I still only know a handful of my friend's last names. When we're referring to a certain Sasha or a particular Natasha, we usually say, "You know, the one with the black hair, or the one married to… or Olga with the blonde hair or Sergei that plays the guitar." Our phone list is also the same way. We have descriptions written beside their names in parentheses! There's "Neighbor Natasha," "Piano Lena," "Driver Sasha," and many more. I was talking to a Ukrainian friend about this, and to my surprise, she said she does the same thing! By the way, there is no such thing as a phone book here, and the phone numbers stay with the apartments.

Their choices of names weren't the only thing limited. You pretty much did what every one else did when it came to lots of things. One of their restricted choices had to do with where you vacationed. Most people, during the decades of communist rule, went to the same places to, "rest." Unlike Americans, they actually take time off to rest for their vacation; it's one and the same. Usually Americans need a vacation, after their, "Vacation."

Most people here use to go (and some still do) to a sanitarium for a restful vacation, or if they have health problems. Many hundreds of people would be at these facilities, which are in the woods on the outskirts of every town. There are hundreds of these places, maybe thousands throughout the country. They are very rustic, motel looking buildings. Inside the rooms are just your basic, very uncomfortable beds and awful looking bathrooms.

I don't think the places I've stayed in look dilapidated because they were that old; it's the way they looked when they were new. Not very good workmanship or pride went into these places. I remember every time I'd leave my room in one of these camps, a chunk of plaster would hit the floor when I shut the door. This is normal for these kinds of accommodations. There are always pieces of plaster missing from the walls of the bathrooms too.

In some of these less than lush vacation spots, they just have one huge tiled room with lots of shower heads sticking out of the walls, no separate stalls, no doors, and no curtains. The hot water comes on only once a day for a limited time, so lots of people just go in at once and bathe. The women have a time slot, then the men. Not a place for the inhibited types!

Years ago, when one of our fellow missionaries decided to go with some Ukrainians on **their** vacation, she said she felt like she had spent a week at a concentration camp! But if you asked the natives, they would tell you what a great time they had. It comes down to whatever you're used too. Now when we're in America traveling, we're much easier to please. We can pull into a Motel 6, and we think we're at the Hilton!

Once I was leading a little overnight retreat with about 50 young Ukrainian women. I was the **only** American. It was my first adventure out of Kiev without my husband. My memory of that night is of trying to sleep, in a room that I was sharing with eight others. It was a nicer, privately owned camp, but the beds were awful. I had the bottom of a bunk bed, which consisted of a very thin, cotton mattress held up by a wire, mesh, springy thing. When I laid in it, my whole body was almost totally resting on the floor! It sank right in the middle; there was mattress on both sides of my face. I looked like a human hotdog! I was awake all night. There weren't enough sheep in the world to get me through that night! I was counting the hours to daylight, not only since I couldn't sleep, but I had needed to go to the bathroom for hours but wasn't about to grope my way through the pitch dark to get to the bathroom. It was some where down the hall, then down some stairs. I didn't want to cause a ruckus. So I just laid there, listening to one gal talk in her sleep. Too bad I couldn't understand her Russian!

Not only are the retreat places the same, so are their apartments. Until independence, all the apartments inside a particular building would have the same light fixtures, wallpaper, and flooring. You would even find the same wallpaper in another building across town. They would have a certain paper and paint, so since this was all they had, it was used every where. Once we were stripping wallpaper off our walls, down to many different layers of paint, and a Ukrainian friend knew which decades each color had been used in.

Communism seems to be a, "One size fits all," kind of government, except for those in power; they get whatever they want. It's nice to see people remodeling their apartments now and being able to pick out what **they** want. They can choose for themselves; no more, "cookie cutter" décor.

CHAPTER 5

HUNTING AND GATHERING

When I first arrived in this foreign land, it was all I could do to put a meal on the table. Having to shop every day and carry it home was fun at first, for the first few days, and then it became work. We didn't and still don't have a car, so I would buy all I could carry, which was about enough for one meal. I soon learned that there was no profit in making a menu first. You shopped first, and then decided what you're going to cook according to what you found. Still to this day, I have trouble getting every thing I need. I usually have to go to several stores to find certain things. I never prayed to find certain food items in America. If you want or need something, it's usually there. Now I'm often praying for items, especially after I've already committed myself to making a certain menu by buying part of it at one store and hoping to find the rest of it at another!

The Outdoor Markets

The open markets were the best place to shop the first few years we were here and still are for fresh fruits and vegetables. We had a huge market right down the street from our apartment and I went there quite few times a week. It was nice until winter came. I always felt sorry for all the vendors out in the snowy, cold weather. I felt sorry for me too when I had to shop in it. They have to brush off snow from their tables, so you can see what they were selling.

You never knew what you might see at the market. I especially hated going into the meat market area. People had chunks of what-ever animal laid out on tables for your viewing. You could tell what was what by looking at whatever animal head might be hanging above or behind the table; a cow's head here, a pig's head over there. I would just point at some meat and ask how much it was; they'd weigh it and put it in a bag. There would be dogs walking around too. Notice I said walking, **not** on the tables for sale! They were just looking for a free bone or two.

I'd never seen fresh rabbit all gutted and ready for cooking. They lay them out on the table and the fir is left on the feet, (maybe so you can make a lucky key chain!) You couldn't get ground beef; you had to grind it yourself. I got a manual meat grinder, which was really hard work. It didn't take me long to say, "Forget this!" We didn't eat much besides chicken those first few years. I'm surprised we didn't just become vegetarians! I was so glad when the day came when we got stores that had meat wrapped and dated just like stores back home.

There are always ladies selling different goods in and around the subway stations, bus stops and anywhere there's lots of people passing through, all hours of the day up until 11:00 at night. There isn't much turnover in personnel in the spots where they have set up their merchandise. I've seen the some of the same people in the same spots for ten years. They are very territorial too. If you're a new person on the block, you may have to go to another block that's got a free space. It's a social event for these people. They sell year after year with the same people, they're like family.

It never ceases to amaze me the variety of stuff one Babushka might have for sale. She'll have a bucket of homemade slaw, a few pairs of underwear, some hammers and maybe some toilet paper! I'm not sure how they decide or how they get their selection, but it's always interesting just to view it as you walk by.

Once I was out shopping and wanted to buy some crackers. So many times I wouldn't know how to convey what I wanted, like how to ask for a certain amount of grams or half of something. They only had crackers in bulk, so you asked for a certain amount. It was different using the metric system, and I didn't know my numbers in Russian yet, so I went ahead and asked for a kilo (a kilogram), which is 2.2 pounds) of crackers. Do you know how many these light weight crackers you'll get if you ask for a kilo? A whole lot of crackers! I needed crackers to take to a picnic, but not everyone in Kiev would be there!

As I mentioned, it's the metric system, and they love weighing stuff! It's never three for $1.00 or $1.00 each around here! They even weigh the watermelons and heads of lettuce! I just want to scream and say, "Just put a sign on the bin, they're all the same size, forget the weighing! I am starting to see some pre-weighed things popping up; bags of apples and such.

When we first arrived, and even now in the market, you can buy just one of something out of a pack. If you just need one battery, they'll open a pack, and sell you just one. Want one cigarette? Sure, no problem. It's great for people who don't have a lot of money and really only need one of something.

I can still remember the first time we got certain things: eggs in a carton. I used to get my eggs from a lady off a truck, or buy them from a babushka who sat on the corner. I had brought my own egg carton from the States and handed it to her to put her fresh farm eggs in to. She thought the carton was very interesting. It took her a minute to figure out how to open it, and then she was puzzled by the twelve spots. They sell eggs by ten here, kind of goes with the metric system I guess. A dozen must be an American thing. I haven't seen a dozen of anything this side of the ocean.

The day we could get chicken breasts was another memorable moment. Before, we only had whole chickens or leg quarters. I always wondered what happened to the rest of the chicken that went with the quarters. One day it finally showed up. The only choice was boneless and skinless which was great and it was cheaper than America. Well, it used to be cheaper.

When any of us would see something for the first time, we would get on the phone and joyfully share our find with fellow missionaries. I'll never forget the day white toilet paper hit the stores. You would (and still do) email home about such events! Once I found several boxes of Kellogg's Cocoa Krispies and almost fainted. Of course I bought all they had (all three boxes) and bragged to others about my great find. This didn't last, before too long the supply was gone and has been seen no more. It remains to be a safe bet to buy something when you see it, especially when it's something you're surprised you found. If you dare hesitate, the one and only one of what you found will be gone. You have to get it when you see it, because most likely you'll never see it again.

It seems like when I'm shopping in America, that when I need help I can't find someone, and when I don't, there are all these people available. Here there seems to be plenty of people working, but they can only work in **their** spot in the store. I'm talking about the little stores that are only about five feet by twelve. They only have a few feet they work in. If there are ten people standing in a line in front of where the bread is, and no one standing in the candy section, the candy lady can't help with the bread. Many times I've been in a line and watched several ladies just standing there waiting on no one. If you ask them for help, they point to the appropriate clerk.

In some of the small neighborhood stores and the bigger department stores, you have to tell the clerk what you want from behind the counter. She then gives you a slip of paper with the price written on it. The next step is to take it to the cashier, who is sometimes clear across the store. You get a receipt from her showing that you paid for your item and finally you return to the first clerk, give her your receipt, and she'll give you what you came for. I get tired just telling you about it! During my first encounter with this, I was kindly led through the process as a clueless foreigner. I caught on real fast!

Wow! Grocery Carts!

When we got our first American type grocery store, we couldn't believe our eyes. We were about to hyperventilate as we walked into this bright and beautiful store. We were so used to the cave-like atmosphere of the communist stores, the brilliant lighting was almost more than we could bear.

We could hardly handle the excitement when we saw grocery carts! Most Ukrainians bought stuff on a daily basis, so they didn't need carts. My friend had driven her car, so we were there to do some serious shopping. People stared at us as our carts began to fill, and as we moved on to load our second ones. It was embarrassing when people started not only staring, but pointing and talking about us. They probably thought we were stocking up a bomb shelter or something!

When we checked out, people were in shock at the amount of money we had spent. We were thrilled with the amount, since we had gotten a lot more for our money than if we had gotten two carts worth in America.

I started bagging my groceries as the cashier was checking me out. Boy! Did being my own bag boy get attention! They had never seen anyone do this before; usually you put your stuff back into your basket or cart and go over to a table and bag it. I'm thinking, "Why would I want to handle this stuff a couple of extra times when I can bag as I check out." Well, the store security guard, who hangs out between the customers and the door, came over next to me and watched, fascinated by this process.

One time I was checking out with my overflowing cart of groceries just chocked full of things no one around me seemed to be buying, and there was a woman and her daughter in front of me. They kept turning their heads staring; the daughter even pointing at my cart. Well, I just couldn't take it any more and blurted out **in English** "It's a lot of stuff, isn't it!" So there! I had gotten it off my chest. Well, I felt like such an idiot as I realized they weren't just thinking "What a crazy American," they were probably saying it as they walked away using their hands, **signing** to each other! They were deaf! Unless they were good at reading English speaking lips, they didn't have a clue to what I had just said!

Shopping in Kiev is just so different than in South Carolina. I always feel at home when I go back to S.C., where I get called honey, sweetie, or sugar several times a day in Wal-Mart or at the gas station. The South is just a friendly place! People usually talk to each other while standing in line, and the cashier asks, "How ya doin'," Even if she really doesn't care how you're doing, at least she asked and you can reply, "Fine," even if you're doing terrible. It's just the customary thing to do. Here, it would blow my mind if a cashier asked me about my well being! All you get it is, "Do you need a bag? Do you have the exact change?" And by the way, the bags aren't free and the thing with the exact change really bugs me! They will ask you every time! It must be a law or something! They seem to have problems keeping enough change in the cash drawers. When we first got here, if they were a few cents short in change, they'd give you a stick of gum or bullion cube instead! I'm glad I had a Ukrainian with me the first time I had this happen, or I would have wondered what in the world they were doing. It's been a long time since I've had this happen. I miss the gum.

Not only is the cashier's attitude different at the checkout, but so is the merchandise on those low lying checkout shelves. Those last minute purchases aren't just for gum any more. My teenage daughter calls them "The Four Cs." You've got your coffee, candy, cigarettes, and condoms! That's right, a little different than what you're use to at your check out I bet. Picture this: your toddler is grabbing stuff and gets a few packs of the last "C," mentioned. What do you do? You've got to put them all back where they go! Meantime, your kid's pitching a fit over some interesting packs of **candy** you won't let him have! If it was me, I'd quickly replace what he had with some candy and get out of there! This could really get some conversation going when you're shopping with your pre-teen; you know that "little talk," you've been putting off? Well, go ahead and get it over with.

Also in the stores, people don't automatically move out of your way. I don't think they have peripheral vision here! I feel stupid when saying excuse me and nothing happens. Where I come from, people are always excusing themselves when trying to get by, and they haven't even touched me yet! Their always apologizing for blocking your view of an item or having to reach any where near you to get something. It took me a while to get use to the difference in shopping etiquette. Southerners are just too nice I guess!

I Shop at Pharmacy # 45, What About You?

In daily life, I see such a difference in the way they've lived here. For example: when you pass a drug store or a school, they just have a number on them; Drugstore # 45 or school # 112. It's so weird not seeing a store name like, "Walgreen's," or a school with a name like, "South Florence High School." Also, until recent years, a truck may pass you and read "Milk," or "Bread." That's all it said. No company name or eye catching logo. Now, with all the imported goods, there are a lot more colorful delivery trucks; also a ton of billboards and advertisements, even to the point of tackiness, but this has brightened things up a lot.

Being the multi-talented shopper I am, I not only draw pictures, but I play charades too! I've acted a few things out over the years, but I had to draw the line at certain products. There are some things you just don't do charades for. Thank goodness the hemorrhoid medicine is pronounced almost the same as in English. All I had to do was ask, **not** act! You see, here, you have to ask for everything at the pharmacy. You can't buy any medicine, even aspirin, at the grocery store.

All the drugs are behind the counter; you can't get them yourself. Most of the medicines are displayed in glass cases, so at least I can read the Russian or point to it if I see what I want. You don't have to have a prescription for antibiotics or most medicines. It's great if you know what you need, but it does seem weird that you can get these drugs and the pharmacist doesn't ask you a single question. If you have a question, you better ask them or if you can read Russian or Ukrainian, then help yourself to some informative reading. The drugs come in their original box (rarely in a bottle) with the extensive, product information about it inside. I wouldn't understand this stuff even if it was in English, so I'd better know what I'm getting!

Pirated Goods and Quality

When it comes to pirated or counterfeited goods, Ukraine is one of the leading nations. No where in America have I seen such items as these. At first I didn't notice any difference because everything else looked the same; logos, colors, etc. When I took a closer look at the spelling, I saw Ree**book,** Adi**dos,** and **M**ike athletic shoes, and To**nn**y Hilfiger shirts. I still wish I had bought the reversible windbreaker I had seen in the market the first year I was here. It was Reebok on one side and Nike on the other! Maybe this was a joint venture I hadn't heard about; neither had these companies!

Since it seemed the quality of goods here was quite low, I learned early on how to say, "This doesn't work." I think there are some companies who have defective products and when they realize it, they put it in the Ukraine bound box! Being the spoiled American that I am, I had high expectations of the products I bought, especially the appliances. In the first few years, I went through two or more of the following: toasters, microwaves, hair dyers, washing machines, coffee makers, and **four** vacuum cleaners! When I was taking my toaster back to the corner store, I repeated to myself the Russian words for, "*it doesn't work,*" over and over, so by the time I got to the counter I hadn't forgotten how to tell them what my problem was. I said it with pride and the clerk, who was used to me coming in clueless, was quite impressed with my Russian! I'll never forget this word; I still have to use it more than I like.

You can always tell by the price or the quality if something is real or not. It seem like most of their clothing is this very cheaply made, overpriced, Chinese stuff. I'll find something, look at the size, and it'll say XXL, but it's still too small for me. They figure since it fit the largest Chinese person they could find, they labeled it as such, but most Chinese are the size of an American small.

I bought one of my son's a, "Nike," windbreaker; the zipper broke the first day. At this time, I didn't know if I could try and take it back to the market or not. Another time I bought my daughter a coat from an indoor market. Most places, until recently, were dimly lit and you couldn't see what you're buying. When I got outside in the light, I could see seams coming apart already, so I went back inside, showed the vender and she gave me my money back. I had such a victorious feeling! I had already been picking up pieces of my daughter's other coat. Buttons and other stuff would fall off as she walked in front of me. I really wanted to find a coat that would stay in one piece for longer than a day! We have a lot of second-hand clothing stores, so if we need something before we get back to the States, we can get used, even American brand clothes, that are much better quality.

One of the funniest of the pirated goods is movies. When we first arrived, back in the days of videos, we were amazed how movies that had just come out in America were already on the streets here for sale. Someone in the States would film the big screen with their video camera while the actual movie was playing in the theater. Not only was the quality bad, but you could see rows of people's heads and watch them getting up to get popcorn! But what do you expect for a few dollars? Back then, there weren't even any official copies for sale. As time has gone on, the quality has gotten much better. Now they just steal the actual movie and make DVDs from that. It's always ironic to start a movie and see the "**FBI Warning**" come up.

What a deterrent! Sometimes you can get six or more movies on one disc. You can find just about anything on the street before it's out in America, but we can also buy "real" DVDs in the stores now; at least I think they're real?

It was always scary to have our computer worked on, until we found someone we really trusted. There are all kinds of pirated computer software and games available. There are dozens on one disc. Back in the early days, we had some guy come over to fix something on our computer, and he offered to install the latest Microsoft software that hadn't even come out in America yet! Imagine that! We declined his offer. He didn't quite seem like the sort of guy who had been given any authority from Bill Gates!

I have come to figure out that some products we stumble upon must have originally been part of a humanitarian aid box or something, because they were the **real** thing. I once bought a pair of mittens that had a Wal-Mart tag on them, priced at $10, but I bought them for $3. I also bought some pajamas with a Sears tag. Churches and organizations need to be careful who they entrust their humanitarian aid with. It can easily end up on the street for sale if you don't know who you're giving it to.

Staying in Touch With Your Money

Until the last couple of years, we only had cash that we had brought over from America. There were no ATMs anywhere, and you couldn't use your credit cards. I remembered the commercial saying, "Visa is everywhere you want to be." It didn't take me long to figure out no one wanted to be in Ukraine, except us missionaries.

Now we occasionally use our credit cards in certain stores and the travel agency, but I still have to make sure I have plenty of cash when shopping. We have to change our dollars to Ukrainian money, or we can get Ukrainian money out of the ATM. I was so used to writing checks or using a debit card, that I've forgotten several times to bring cash or get money changed. Usually there is a money changing booth in or near the store. When we first moved over, I had about five items at the check out and had forgotten to bring money. I was embarrassed and didn't know how to tell the clerk I'd be back in a few minutes with money. When I came back in the store, sure enough, they had put my items back on the shelf!

I love shopping when I'm visiting America. I don't have to convert money, have cash, be self conscious about my full cart, or worry about finding certain items. I used to think grocery shopping in America was such drudgery. Here, it feels like such an accomplishment to get it done and in the house. Shopping is so easy in America! And don't you forget it!

Thanksgiving Turkey Hunt

I've been known to draw a few pictures while out shopping, when I didn't know how to tell someone what I was looking for. I call it "Pictionary with a purpose." I think my favorite was my drawing of a turkey. Hey, after my corner butcher looked at my drawing and said the Russian word for it, I never have forgotten the word for turkey! And yes, later on he did have two frozen turkeys for our staff's Thanksgiving dinner! We were some thankful Americans, celebrating Thanksgiving in Ukraine, eating turkeys from France! This beat the turkey sandwich meat they had had the year before we had come! They don't raise turkeys here for their holidays; they're "duck people," when it comes to celebrating. You can go to the grocery store and get a duck any time, but it's been harder to find turkeys until recent years.

One Thanksgiving, our friend Linda had found a babushka in the market that said she would sell us a turkey she had raised out at her little farm house on the outskirts of Kiev. We were excited about having a fresh turkey for Thanksgiving. You can have your Butterballs; we were going for the free range bird! Well the day before the big day, this babushka showed up at Linda's door with the turkey; there she was holding the turkey by its broken neck, feathers and all! We wanted fresh, but not that fresh! Linda was a real trooper and dressed that bird; probably after some consultation from a local on how to do so, or maybe she looked on the internet!

One year, not too long ago, a couple had come in from the countryside and was selling their vegetables on the sidewalk near my apartment, along with all of the other people. It was about two weeks before Thanksgiving, and I was commissioned to find the turkey for our staff dinner. Well, I already had my radar up and running and all of the sudden, there it was, a huge turkey, already dressed and nowhere to go! This couple standing there selling this beautiful bird had no idea they were the answer to a missionary's prayer. Don't you see what you're missing? Have you ever prayed to find a turkey for Thanksgiving?

I'd never seen a turkey this big, and I can't believe they thought a Ukrainian was going to ever buy it. You see, they charge about $3 per pound for a turkey. But who cared, I was a rich American looking for a Thanksgiving Day turkey. Someone must have tipped them off about me living in the neighborhood and that we had a holiday coming up. I think they were waiting just for me! When I turned the corner and saw that bird, it glowed like I had found the end of the rainbow and the pot had **my** name on it! I wish now I had been more thankful on all those Thanksgiving Days in America.

CHAPTER 6

THE CUSTOMER IS ALWAYS RIGHT, RIGHT?

I think Communism is to blame for most of what seems weird to us here. Hopefully some of this baggage will be taken away in the future, but it's not going to happen over night. They were so used to doing exactly what they were told, it's hardly a place where you hear the phrases "You deserve a break today," or "Have it your way." Customer service and marketing skills haven't quite developed yet.

When I first got here, I had to get used to the interesting store hours that some shops kept. They break for lunch for an hour sometime between 1:00 and 3:00. You have to remember which stores have what break. They could have half of the employees work while the others have lunch and not miss any customers, but they don't see it this way. I am always aggravated when I forget the break time and have to wait.

You never know what hours people work in some jobs. I've seen the garbage truck emptying out the dumpsters at 11:00 on Sunday night. If ever I am up during the wee hours of the morning, I'll look out the window and see what's going on. You always see a few cars and taxis, but others that work during the night are cement truck drivers. I think they work during the night because there is so much traffic during the day, if they got stuck, so would their cement!

My husband was at the outdoor market one day and stopped by a vendor to get a bite to eat. She was serving up pitas filled with meat and topped off with mayo and slaw. Well, he did the unthinkable and asked for his pita without the slaw. The woman was taken back by this crazy request and said "I can't do that." My husband replied, "Sure you can, just don't put it on there. I'll pay the same amount and everything" The frustrated vendor repeated herself and refused to do it, even though Timmy explained how easy it was NOT to do it! I guess this woman had been pita trained; told **the one** way and **only** way to serve the pita, and she wasn't going to deviate from this! After going around and around, she won the battle. Timmy, having grown hungrier and weakened from the fight, succumbed to her "by the book" pita serving and got it with the slaw, like it or not!

The Lord knew I needed to grow in patience, among other things, so He sent me to Ukraine for a training ground. Here it is ten years later, and I'm still being challenged in this area every day. The Ukrainians are so used to waiting in line, because during communism there were many times they had to wait for hours to meet their daily needs. They have this waiting in line down to an art form. You need to be trained in the line waiting protocol before entering the country.

You wouldn't believe how the lines form; most of the time they're not straight in front of a counter as you would think they should be. They go down by the side of the counter or wall, and if you're not in the line correctly, then you're just simply out of luck. There have been many times when I thought I was fifth in line only to find out I'm eighth or tenth. The rule is as follows: if you have something else to do, you can ask the person in front or back of you to hold your place, then you can return later. I've never asked anyone to hold my place, but I've held many a person's place. I understand what they are asking me, even though I don't know how to say it in Russian myself. I've witnessed many a harsh word when someone breaks protocol and mistakenly tries to go ahead of someone out of order. Then everyone chimes in with who they think is next.

Sometimes if you're in line to pay your bills or taking care of some other business, you may see twenty people standing in line and then there's the unseen who are having their spots held. Sometimes you think you're never going to reach the front of the line! Then there's the room or hallway full of people. It can get confusing each time a new person enters and asks who is last in line because sometimes there is no actual line; everyone is just standing or sitting around the room. When I'm in this situation and someone ask me who's last, I can get by with a little pointing, a lot of shrugging or just some good ole ignoring.

We've heard that now you can pay your utility and phone bills on line! Who would have ever believed you could do this here? It's too good to be true. I bet some how that I'll still have to wait in line, on line!

There is another phenomenon among some stores here that I've never heard of happening in America; store owners making decisions without asking the customer. For example: you order a couch and you've picked out the style and fabric you want it made in. They deliver your couch a few weeks later and lo and behold, it's not the fabric you picked out! When you ask them what's up with the fabric, they tell you "Oh, we didn't have that one in stock any more, so we picked another out for you." Can you imagine the look on a person's face, better yet an American's face, when they're told this? I've heard a story like this several times. They even tried to pull one over on me with my kitchen cabinets. We had bought an apartment instead of renting, and had to do some remodeling. I ordered new cabinets, and when they started bringing them in, I realized right away these weren't the cabinets I had ordered! I had them march right back to the truck with them and reorder the right ones. I was surprised to get a call from the salesman, reassuring me that I would have the right ones soon.

Another friend of mine, Neva, had picked out and ordered some tile for her home, and it was to be picked up and installed while she was visiting her family in America. Well, she arrived back in Ukraine, got to her house and there the tile was, installed beautifully. There was only one catch; it was the wrong tile! The tile store didn't have the one she ordered in stock, so they took the liberty of picking out something else for her! When her tile guy picked it up from the store, he had no idea it wasn't what she had ordered and installed it.

When I was ordering a couch, I had bought the fabric at one place and was getting the couch made at another. Most of the time here, they push all their furniture up against the wall, because they don't have enough room in their small apartments to arrange them loosely. Well, when I told them I wanted the back of my couch covered in fabric also, they looked at me like I was crazy; why waste fabric on a place you wouldn't see, since it would be against the wall. I went on to explain to them that my sofa would be out in the room, not against the wall; they tried to convince me otherwise. This really gave them something to talk about the rest of the day.

Taking liberties too far

One woman took her liberty way too far when babysitting an American's toddler. When my friend returned home, there was her one year old little girl with her new hair cut! The Ukrainian woman took it upon herself to cut this child's hair, because she thought it needed to be cut! It had never been cut too. Can you imagine someone you just met giving your baby girl her first hair cut without your permission! My friend, who couldn't believe her eyes, tried to calmly explain why this didn't, "cut it," according to American culture. One summer, some missionaries were home in America and lent their van to some Ukrainians while they were gone. When they got back to Kiev, the seatbelts in their van were gone! They asked their friends what happened to them, they replied, "Oh, we cut them out. You don't need them."

Once I was shopping for an air-conditioner that you put in your window. These window units were hard to come by then, but after looking in many stores, I finally found what I needed. I didn't see a price, so I asked a clerk for help. He looked all over it and didn't see a tag. He said he didn't know the price. I asked him to please find out. He said the manager was the only one that knew, and the manager wasn't there. When I asked when the manager would be back, he said next week; he was in Moscow. There was no one else that could help, and he didn't seem too worried about losing a sale. I could sure tell he didn't work on commission! I questioned the Lord on this, as I often do when things aren't working out as **I** think they should . Usually the Lord has something better for me, and He did. He led me to another store where I found the perfect air-conditioner and for a great price too.

The Lord has saved me many times from buying the wrong thing. Once I was buying a refrigerator and was about to use my credit card when the computer went down. I couldn't get it. I wondered what the Lord was doing. Well, I came back the next week and was about to buy it again when I saw a section of appliances that I hadn't seen before; the scratch and dent section.

I looked and found exactly what I was looking for, and it was a much better brand than the one I was about to buy. I asked what was wrong with it; it looked brand new. The clerk said it had just been used a few months. That's why it was there. I couldn't believe the price. It was less than half its original price. So I thanked the Lord for the technical difficulty (blessed inconvenience) that turned into a blessing.

Sometimes stores will have something on display, but not actually have the product or they're out of it. They should take the sample out of the display case or off the counter if they're out, but they don't. I've seen stores that have a NIKE sign in the window, but don't sell Nike products; it's just for decoration. Once the Nesquick bunny was out in front of a store handing out flyers, but the store didn't have any Nesquick!

They used to not have sales here after the season was done, but they have finally got around to it, it's great! The signs read 7% off! Not youre usual 25% or 50%. It's always some weird number. They still don't sell by seasons. The mosquito repellent is still on display through the winter as if it was summer. You can still get some Christmas wrapping paper about anytime, and if you missed Valentine's Day, don't worry, I've seen them stocking the shelves with new Valentine's items a week after the holiday!

One day I went into a convenience store and got a Coke and a bottle of iced tea. I put the two bottles on the counter; the clerk rang up the Coke, but put the iced tea on the counter behind him. I said that I wanted the ice tea too. He mumbled something to me and wouldn't give it to me. There was a whole refrigerated case of the tea right behind me; was it all poison? Why wouldn't he give me the tea! Why not remove all the tea in that case if it wasn't for sale! I left tea-less and still wonder to this day why I couldn't have it. This happened again another day in another store. They wouldn't sell me a certain flavor of Capri Sun. They let me have several of one flavor, but none of another. We couldn't understand why we couldn't have it, especially since it was **in the store for sale!**

This leads me to the overall lack of customer service here. You know how in America you usually get one of two kinds of sales people: the over zealous, hyper ones who are on commission or the laid back type that say "Let me know if you need anything." I rather have the latter, but here in Ukraine, you get neither. You can walk in most stores and be on your own throughout your shopping experience. Now if you're suspicious looking to them or you're a kid, you'll be followed from a distance and stared at the whole time. One of my sons went into a store, but left because they didn't have what he needed. As soon as he walked out the door, two plain-clothes security guards grabbed him by the arm and began to frisk him! Just the other day, someone told me that they weren't allowed to take their four year old in the store with them; she wasn't old enough! This is a German owned store similar to our Sam's Ware-house. I've never heard of a rule like this anywhere. I can see not letting little kids in unaccompanied by an adult, but with parents? I asked a German friend about this rule, and she said it wasn't that way at this same store in Germany.

Just the other day, after shopping for years in this store, I was stopped by the guard at the entrance, because I hadn't checked my tote bag in at the desk. There's a woman working at this post where you can put a bag or items that you don't want or can't take into the grocery store. There are numbered cuvee holes like this in most stores. I didn't have anything in my bag, which was the point! I brought it with me, so I could fill it up with my purchases. I do this all the time. But the guard who was consumed with his authority and power wouldn't let me take it in. I tried to tell him I do this every day, but he said, "That was before." So being the law abiding, non-Ukrainian, non citizen that I am, I got into the line, and checked my empty bag in. Then after I had unloaded my hand basket of goods at check out, picked them back up, and then put them back into my hand basket, so I could get in line to retrieve my empty bag from the cuvee hole lady! The very next day I had to get something else from this store, and Barney Fife wasn't working that day. The guy on duty didn't even notice when I proudly walked in with my empty bag. You've got to love the consistency here!

When it comes to making appliance or furniture purchases, it's a very big deal. No matter how big or how small, there is so much paperwork involved. If it's electrical, it's going to take you even longer to get out of the store. In most stores, if you're buying a toaster, television, refrigerator, or anything else, it's got to be taken out of the box, unwrapped and plugged in to show you it works. I get so annoyed at this. I just want to take my purchase and go! You've got all the wrap, styrofoam, and cardboard every where; then it's got to go back in the box the way it came. Yeah, right! And then there's the stamping! You have all these documents and warranties that have to be stamped or papers that have to be hand copied. You've never seen anything quite like it.

Getting a big purchase home is a challenge, if the store doesn't have delivery. Back in our early years here, this was always a problem. It wasn't like we could call a friend and borrow their pick-up truck; which in the south is about every friend you have. I have found all kinds of ways to get stuff to my apartment. When it's just a few blocks away, I've carried stuff home myself. At different times, I've been seen carrying a roll of linoleum, carpet, and a coffee table to name a few and I've passed people carrying toilets and other things on my way. I've also assisted and walked alongside men who've I paid to carry tables, stoves, and mattresses.

I've ridden in countless cars and trucks with guys bringing home all kinds of things. I had to help take a huge piece of countertop up to our apartment. We needed it in one piece and it wouldn't fit in the elevator. We live on the eighteenth floor; what a workout!

Our previous apartment was on the first floor, so when we moved to our eighteenth floor place, I didn't think of what might not fit in the elevator. We had had an extra long couch made for our old place and it wouldn't fit in the elevator. Two guys brought it up, and after eighteen flights, they were still smiling when they reached my door! I felt so bad for them and apologized. They said it was no problem.

In America, I imagine it would cost so much to have a couch brought up eighteen flights. You might as well go buy a new, smaller couch! Here most of the furniture comes apart just for this reason; tall buildings with small elevators. It seems like the things we've had to take apart have never been the same since. They seem to be less sturdy after each move. I really hate seeing pianos being brought up in parts. At least we haven't had that problem. The first floor was good for having a piano, and our big elevator saved the day at our new place.

My mom visited us a few months after we moved, and we went out shopping for a mattress. We found one right in a store on our corner. I saw a guy in our neighborhood that had a big truck, so we asked him if he'd go to the corner and get the mattress for us. I knew very little Russian at that time, but the word for mattress was the same-only pronounced like a Brit would say it. I knew the word for home and pointed to mine. After a few moments of charades, I pointed to my watch and we agreed on a time and a payment. He ran home to get Ukrainian money to exchange with me, before I changed my dollars to buy the mattress. They like to keep their savings in dollars, and he could exchange with me without a fee. We had a successful delivery. He was glad to make a little extra money, and I was glad to have a comfortable, new mattress.

When we moved to our second rented apartment, we took our new mattress with us, but we couldn't take the bed because it was the landlord's. Our first apartment came furnished for the most part, but the second one didn't have all the beds we needed. Well we moved, then Timmy had to go out of town for a week. I went shopping and found a bed that fit our mattress, which wasn't easy, since there are more than the three sizes that are in the States.

For a fee, the store delivered it. But what I didn't realize was that this was for the delivery only, and not the assembly. I didn't mind paying more; they usually will do it for some additional loot. Well, this guy said he didn't want to do it. I tried offering him more money than usual, but he didn't care. He left me there with all kinds of pieces, screws, nuts and bolts! I'm pretty good at repairing things, but this was something new, and something new always has instructions. I hate instructions in English, so what was I supposed to do with Russian instructions? Timmy is always the director of the directions in our house, better yet the, "Bi-lingual instruction reader," but he was gone. I started out thinking I could get this bed together with no problems. Ha! I came back to reality real fast! What was I thinking? I had a lapse in memory for a minute, but came back to the realization that I wasn't living in Kansas anymore!

And everything here takes so much longer than you think. Well it turned out to be several hours of torment!" I got it somewhat together and was under it forever trying to get some nuts and bolts on. All you could see were my feet hanging out. I looked just like I was under a car changing the oil!

When we first moved to Ukraine, we were surprised one night when the doorbell rang at 10:30 and there was this little old lady (a Babushka) standing there. She handed us our electric bill! She was making her rounds with her plastic grocery bag, handing out the mail. This was our mailman! A little different than home, but she got the job done.

There are post offices just about on every street. Once in a while I'll see little yellow mail trucks driving by. The reason I know it's a mail truck is because I saw the driver emptying out a street mailbox one day. Our mailbox is in the entry way of our apartment building, along with the other ninety or so! They're just these skinny metal slots that you open with a key. Well, we don't open ours with a key, because the former owner didn't leave it with us! Since this group of boxes just hangs loosely on the wall, I just pull our section of boxes away from the wall and pull our mail out from the back. I guess the keys really don't do a whole lot of good, do they?

The post office is always an interesting place with which to interact. We don't get much mail, except for the monthly bills, but sometimes we get these little scrap pieces of paper with a hand written note scribbled on them. It wasn't until we asked someone about it, and found out it was from the post office. We usually don't understand exactly what it is saying, but Timmy goes down the street to get whatever they have for us that wouldn't fit in our mailbox. Once some of our friends got one of these scribbled scraps and asked us what it was. We recognized it right away and told them what to do. They had had it a while, and were getting other notes complaining about them not coming to get it. They even got a phone call from the post office. They were all out of sorts because our friends had not picked up this package for days, and it was taking up too much space at the post office; it was in the way! Our friends were puzzled and somewhat excited to get down there and see what huge package they were receiving. They got there, showed the P.O. worker their passports for ID, and they brought it out. This huge thing that they were so upset about taking up there space was a shoebox! No wonder the post office was so upset, who has room for such a **big** box?

I recently had a package sent to The Republic of Georgia. It was a box with several things in it. They took everything out and weighed them separately, including the empty box! Then they added it all up and charged me accordingly. Can anyone out there tell me **why** they had to do it this way?

Ukraine has great flowers and they're a lot cheaper than in America. I often receive fresh flowers from my husband, but don't appreciate the question he is often asked when buying them. The flower lady will ask, "Are these for your wife or mistress?" Can you believe this! Can you imagine this being a normally asked question at **your** local florist? It would be interesting to ask and watch their response. I guess you may run across some American man that would say, "None of your business," but not here. Also Timmy has had taxi drivers ask him about his mistress just after he has told them about me and the kids! It's always a good opportunity for Timmy to share God's view on this when asked this horrible question.

Earlier I told you about getting my hair done, but my friend Mindy just told me of her perm experience and I've never heard one like it. Now this is what I call customer service! I think this beautician must moonlight as a bartender! This is her story in her own words:

I decided to get a permanent, and had brought the perm kit from America. All was going smoothly – Oksana (my hairdresser) prepared and inserted the rods, "sponged" the solution carefully on my hair, and then we sat together, waiting for the 20-minute time period to elapse. Oksana tested one of the curls, and I saw a look of concern pass over her face. "Are we using the same permanent that you usually buy?" she asked. When I replied, "Yes," she placed her hands on my head, and then exclaimed: "Oh, your head is not warm enough – it is much too cold! The perm will not work with your head this cold!" She barked out instructions to her co-worker, and before I knew it, a LARGE glass of cognac had been placed

72

into my hand, along with a piece of chocolate. "Drink," she said, "Drink all of it." "I haven't really had much to eat today," I replied. "Even better," she answered. "You must drink all of it, or the perm will not work properly."

Under the circumstances, I felt that I really had no option but to comply, so I slowly drank the entire glass of cognac, and placed it on the counter. Oksana waited a few minutes more, then took the rods out of my hair. "Ahhhh....," she sighed, "the cognac worked, and your permanent is wonderful! Next time, we will give you another glass of cognac, and just leave the solution on for 15 minutes!" There were smiles of relief all around, and I left the salon, warm and curly! Another day at the salon in Ukraine!

After my friend's perm episode, I really worry about trying to get another perm here. But I guess as long as I don't, "perm and drive," I'll be ok!

CHAPTER 7

KNOCK ON WOOD, SERIOUSLY!

In America we knock on wood just as much as anybody I guess, but I've never put any weight in it. Not so in Ukraine! I've not been in any other cultures long enough to know if they take their superstitions seriously, but it didn't take me long to know what I was dealing with here. I've noticed friends or neighbors don't tell you something their anticipating happening, because it's bad luck to do so and then it won't happen. You don't do things ahead of time like: giving wedding gifts before the wedding, baby gifts before the baby arrives, or giving birthday presents or wishes early. I broke this rule once by having a baby shower, which was a new thing for them anyway. I was thankful everything turned out all right, since I had told them it was just a silly superstition and that I'd been a part of these kinds of parties for years.

Don't ever hand someone something over the threshold of a doorway. I've been chewed out for this by many a Babushka over the years. Believe me! You haven't been really chewed out until you've been chewed out in Russian and don't know what they've said! I try to remember to have them step inside the door or for me to step outside, when all I've wanted to do is just hand them something or get something from them. Why do they have to make a federal case out of it! And I still don't know what's supposed to happen to me when I mess this one up!

Also, whatever you do, don't whistle indoors! If you do, you won't have any money! I will purposely do this just to show them it's not true. I guess they think since I'm an American, I'm immune from this curse! Also if someone sweeps with a broom around a young girl's feet, she'll be an old maid.

Another tip, watch out for those satellite dishes; they'll make you sick! Our friend Becky had gotten a satellite dish, but her side of the building was not facing the right direction for reception. She asked one of her babushka neighbors if she could have it hung on her side of the apartment building and she agreed. About a week or so later, her neighbor got sick, and someone told her it was the satellite dish; she believed this and made Becky take it down. Now I guess if you have a dish you're wondering if you should switch to cable.

When you're out shopping and get to the checkout, you'll notice that the cashiers usually have a small dish or tray to put your change in and you take it out of that. They hardly ever put it directly in your hand. I've noticed this when asking them to pass such a thing as a salt shaker too. They put things down first, not in your hand. Sometimes I'm not sure if something is a superstition or a tradition, but I think most of them are related.

Let's not forget the one about sitting on cold, concrete or marble steps. Did you know this will make you sterile? There are all kinds of dangers I was unaware of until I moved to Ukraine!

Just the other day, my daughter Laurel and her friends were at the beach along the river. It wasn't summer yet, but a cool spring day. After two of the guys had waded in the river and gotten their pants wet, when along came a babushka full of medical advice. She told Jo, one of the wet young men who were sitting, that he shouldn't being sitting in wet britches on the cold ground, because he would get prostate cancer! My daughter had an interesting discussion with her about this, but you never win these debates. Jo, who was just visiting, learned an important cultural truth, "There's no sense arguing with a babushka," not to mention some incredible medical advice to take home to America!

Also cold drinks will give you a sore throat and whatever you do, don't drink one if you already have a sore throat! I've heard of several cultures who believe this. Being from the south, my veins have flowed with iced tea my whole life and I've never had a problem with sore throats! I think this myth is on its way out because not only are we seeing people won to Christ, we're having many conversions to iced tea too! Some of them even want ice cubes in their tea. Cold drinks are becoming more popular with the younger generation.

When we first got here, you couldn't get a cold drink anywhere. If we were out, I got used to drinking a hot Coke. I remember when a

Ukrainian saw me emptying some ice trays that I had brought from the States; she said "That's so cool." That was in 1998, and it wasn't long before you could get ice trays here. I don't known of a Ukrainian who uses ice trays, but there must be some out there who do.

Speaking of ice, it's strange that they're scared of drinking cold drinks, while others here think it's healthy to jump into the frozen river or dump a bucket of cold water over your head! The jolt is supposed to be good for you! One wintry day, Timmy was walking along the river front having a quiet time. The next thing he knew, a woman coming out of the river without a stitch! Talk about a jolt! He quickly made a u-turn and continued his walk elsewhere.

Another big no-no is being in or causing a draft! This can start an all out war. Even if you think the heat will kill you while on a crowded bus or any other transportation, beware when opening a window. If there are windows open already on one side, you can't open windows on the other to create a draft. Hey, I don't like a draft blowing on me when I'm cold, but come on, when it's hot you've got to get some air moving. Not here you don't! I've cracked a window in front of me on the bus several times only to see a hand slide it right back into the closed position. You're about to die, but no one else seems to care as the beads of sweat start trickling down your face. We've seen verbal and close to physical fights start over this. Drafts will make you sick, period! So don't get caught creating one. They sell fans and air-conditioners, but it seems like every time we've got ours on, and Ukrainians are over, they turn them off.

Another interesting superstition is one of religious nature. Icons, which are very ornate pictures of Mary, Jesus and different saints, are a big thing here because of the Orthodox Church. They come in all shapes and sizes and are seen throughout the city not only in the churches, but in all kinds of places. Most buses and taxi drivers will have them on or above their dashboard. This is to, "protect," them. Once I was in a taxi and he asked me, as many do, why I was in Kiev. After telling him I was a missionary, he quickly reached over and pulled a Bible out of the glove compartment. I hadn't found a fellow believer, but someone who believed keeping a Bible in his glove compartment was protecting him from a car accident.

One day, I heard a car as it raced up to a store and came to a squealing halt. They had loud music playing and all kinds of stickers on the back windshield. I looked to see what kind of interesting clientele was about to enter the store. To my surprise, it was two monks (or priests) from the monastery! They got out wearing their long, thick, itchy-looking, wooly robes, got some ice cream from the lady vendor out front and then took off. I thought to myself, "Boy! Things sure have changed! What happen to the vow of silence and all that stuff?" I guess this was the new generation from the monastery. Since they drove the way they did, I wondered how many Bibles and icons it was taking to protect **them**, or did they have automatic coverage?

Here's an interesting quirk that deals with flowers. We have flowers for sale everywhere, and when you buy flowers from a shop or vender on the street, you can't buy a dozen red roses or a dozen of anything except for one reason.! You can get eleven or thirteen, but not twelve. Now if the flowers are for a funeral, you can buy twelve. Even number of flowers are for funerals, odd for every thing else! They are serious about this too. Someone once brought me flowers for my birthday, but one of the stems was broken, so they had to take another flower out of the bouquet to make it odd number. I ended up losing two flowers! Now I did get the other single flower, but we had to put it in a vase by itself. I've been to Ukrainian homes and seen the extra vase with the same flower in it many times.

Also the horoscope is very popular and taken seriously. I read the other day in a Ukrainian article where they believed the suicide rate had gone up because of certain astrological events! I know this is somewhat true in America as well, when it comes to the horoscope, but here no one is telling them otherwise.

I think the area of superstitions is one that really needs to be addressed, even among the believers here. Old habits are hard to break, but Christ can break these patterns of thinking.

CHAPTER 8

IT'S A BEAUTIFUL DAY IN THE NEIGHBORHOOD...

When we first moved to Kiev, we rented an apartment and continued to do so for about three years, and then we bought our own apartment. I was used to a large home, so when we moved to Ukraine I had to get used to smaller quarters. We had an older home in Clemson with 3500 square feet. We had lots of room to entertain and have fellowship. Well, our first apartment was about 800 square feet which was considered a big apartment in Kiev. We survived and packed people in for fellowship wherever they would fit. Our next apartment was about the same size, but laid out a little better. Later we bought two smaller apartments that had been joined as one; we moved up to 1000 square feet. Then four years later, we sold that one and found an unusual two-story apartment with 1500 square feet. They rarely make apartments with more than 1000 square feet, so we're very blessed to have this much room. We're able to do a lot of ministry in our home.

There are several styles of apartments: old brick, old concrete, and old brick or tile covered concrete. Some of them aren't really that old, they just look old. They seemed to have been neglected and run down, but they didn't look too great even when they were brand new. The communists didn't have much taste or imagination. They had to suppress it; they were communists! They just threw together some eyesores to house the masses. Until recent years, the apartment building choices were five-story (with no elevator), nine stories (with one small elevator) or eighteen stories (with one small and one large elevator). I can't imagine moving into an apartment on the fifth floor of one of these five story buildings. Carrying the furniture up all those stairs and then carrying your groceries up for years afterwards!

One year, we surprised our son Dawson with a ping pong table for Christmas, knowing we were going to be moving into a bigger apartment that was on the **first** floor. So it took two strong delivery guys to get this thing up six flights of stairs. I felt so bad that we didn't have a big elevator for them to use, and I also would have rather not made such a scene having it brought up the stairs. I know our neighbors were really talking about us that day, thinking, "How in the world are they going to play ping pong in there, those crazy Americans!"

The elevator is usually reliable except on a few occasions when I had some very heavy things to take up! In the early days, before the grocery stores that we have now, I got a lot of things bulk from the market. Well, I decided to order a 100 pound sack of both flour and sugar. The guys I bought it from only bring it to the apartment entrance; you have to take it from there. Wouldn't you know it, the elevator broke that day and we lived on the 7th floor! Well, Timmy and our friend Scott had to take these heavy loads up seven flights. I thought they were going to die before they got to the door! Other times I've had someone take me to the store, and I've come home with a car full of groceries, only to find out the elevator had broken down while I was gone. What a work out! It was comforting to later see the elevator repairman drive up in his *Otis* service car. It was exciting to see a familiar name from America. I was hoping the elevator was a real Otis brand and not pirated!

Once we had some people over for supper and they had to leave for a meeting afterwards. We also had to go to this meeting, but not as early as Eric and the others. When we left for the meeting and got to the elevator, there our friends were still in the closed elevator. They had been stuck in there an hour and a half! The four of them, which is all it'll hold, were just talking and singing away in the dark! We finally pried the doors open and got them out.

I also got stuck in this same elevator with a guy I didn't know, in the dark! I don't mind thumbing rides with strange men, but being in a dark, tiny elevator with one is different! I asked this guy if he spoke English, he said, "A little." We passed the time trying to talk. I found out he was my neighbor's son, from two floors down. He looked as if he was about twenty years old and after our twenty minute conversation, his dad showed up and got us out. This is one way to meet your neighbors, but not my first choice! I also don't like it when you're in a sixteen story apartment building and the light in the elevator is out. It's creepy when you stop on a lot of floors, people get in and you're riding for that long in the dark.

The apartments also have one or two balconies which people have usually enclosed in a variety of ways, which adds to the inconsistency of the outward appearance of the buildings. There aren't any codes to follow or rules to adhere to (that I'm aware of, or that people follow), and no one from The Better Homes & Garden Club is going to come by and tell you what you can and cannot do! I wonder what my neighbors would think if I told them that in some American neighborhoods, you're not allowed to hang out laundry!

Apartment Sweet Apartment

When we arrived, our kids already knew what to expect their neighborhood to be like, since we had brought them to Ukraine for a trial run the summer before. So entering our ghetto looking apartment building was no shock. It was a nine story, blah, tile covered building that was only thirty something years old, but looked a hundred! The entrance made a less than desirable first impression and the smell was even worse. There was one small elevator, just enough room for our family. It was a tight fit, especially when you're trying your best **not** to touch the walls, especially the inside of the doors! You see, the inside of the doors had blobs of dried, how do I say this, um, dried "stuff" on them, from people's noses! They have a bad habit here of blowing their noses onto things, as opposed to, into things. I asked the kids, "Remember all those shots you had to get before we moved? Well, you got those so you could ride in this elevator!"

You always have to be careful not to touch the walls in any of the buildings or you have white stuff on your hands or your clothes. They have white washed all the walls and this powdery paint just comes right off. It took us a while to get used to this. Many times I would come home, take off my coat and see all this white stuff on the back. I wondered how long I had been walking around being marked, and branded as another foreigner who forgot not to lean on the wall while waiting somewhere. It's really bad when you have a brand new piece of furniture that has to be brought up by the stairs, and it's rubbing against the wall at each tight place and every corner, getting this powder rubbed into the fabric. There' nothing like breaking in the new couch this way!

In our first apartment, the rooms were full of interesting, wallpapered walls, even the ceilings were wallpapered! There were several patterns in each room. My bedroom was made up of four floral designs; the wall, two borders and the ceiling were all different. And after I threw in my floral bedspread and flowery rug, I got dizzy every time I walked in the room! I don't know who in this world first decided what things match and what things don't, but they have a different way of deciding this here, and it's quite different than what I'm used to.

The kitchen was a challenge. I had just one small, bathroom size sink and one old, wobbly cabinet for counter space. This was tough for someone who loved to cook and had had a huge kitchen back in America. I replaced the sink with a double one, bought a new refrigerator, but pretty much lived with the rest. We lived in this place for a little over a year, and then moved across the street to a place that was a little better.

We were blessed to have really good landlords when we were renting, but not every missionary has been as fortunate. Some of our missionary friends have had some terrible experiences with their apartments and landlords. Once, in the middle of the night, one of our friends had their landlord show up with the police and order them to move out, right then! So without warning, they had to wake their kids up and start packing! Even if you have a lease agreement, it's not worth much. Fortunately, they were able to move in to some other missionary's place who happened to be gone for a couple of months and they could have time to find a new place.

You never know when your rent will go up either. We've had friends whose landlords come over and double their rent. One went from $1000 to $2000 a month overnight!

Our friend Laurie was forced out of her place because the landlord was going to get twice as much rent from some guys. These guys had a boss who looked like he just stepped off the set of *The Sopranos!* Who can argue with a landlord who's got the mob breathing down their neck?

Another missionary family was surprised one night by some of their landlord's relatives at the door. This woman announced that this was her father's apartment, and she was moving in. So she and her kids just marched on in and made themselves at home. They ate whatever was there, used whatever appliances they needed; they just took over. There was nothing our friends could do. These unwanted relatives wouldn't get out, so our friends had to.

Also, when you're renting, sometimes people might complain about you having a lot of gatherings at your place. Even though you're not doing anything wrong and it's none of their business, they put the heat on your landlord to get rid of you just because they don't like what you're doing.

Our friends David and Mindy had a bad situation. This is their story: Our first apartment in Kiev was small, but lovely – the landlady had taken care to remodel and decorate it tastefully, and it was just right for the two of us, and for our new Ukrainian friends, as we started having weekly Bible studies, times for tea and cakes, etc. However, it didn't take long for us to realize that **the** major trial of our first year in Kiev would be **the noise**. We lived in one of the many five-story, cheaply constructed apartment buildings, with walls so thin that you could hear the smallest sounds - the televisions, the children crying, the old men snoring, and the babushkas in conversation with one another.

Below us lived a combined family, and between them they had three teenage boys. Every day, as each boy would come home from school, he would crank up his music to an impossible level, so loud that our floors would actually shake. This would happen day and night, and our nerves were soon frazzled. Our knowledge of Russian was almost non-existent, but we looked up the words for "too loud" (we knew the word for music!), and, every day, David would walk downstairs and ask them to turn down the music. Each time a young boy came home, the process would be repeated.

When that did not work, we tried the "neighborly" approach – we baked chocolate chip cookies, and took them to the family, asking them in the nicest way possible if they could keep the music down. They always were pleasant and agreeable, but the music continued. And it was not only the teenagers – the mother and father would often have evening get-togethers, and the drinks were passed around freely. By 11:00 p.m., the rich baritone voice of the father (accompanied by someone on the piano) would fill the air (and our apartment), and sleep was virtually impossible. The situation continued to worsen, and finally, our landlady, desperate to keep us as renters, decided to actually **pay** the people downstairs to be quiet. We did not want her to do so, but she insisted, displaying a common Ukrainian character quality of resignation and acceptance of a difficult situation.

Well, you can see now why it may be better to own your place instead of renting, not only for financial reasons, but for peace of mind. This peace or lack there of, depends on your landlord. We only had a slight problem with our second landlord. The tax police kept coming to our door looking for him. Early in the morning, or late at night, they kept staking out our place waiting for him to show up. They would come to the door and ask for him, and I'd tell them every time, "He doesn't live here. We rent from him." Once they showed me a file, which had his picture on it, asking, "Is this him?" I knew some of the time he was in America and other times I would contact his wife and try to warn her that the police had been by. They usually had already been by her place and her in-laws place too.

The police never asked me if I knew how to contact my landlord, so I never offered. I wasn't sure if these guys were real cops or not; they could have been the bad guys for all I knew. They finally did ask one day if I had a number for him, so I gave it to them. I didn't want to get in trouble in case they were for real. After this landlord decided to sell, we decided to look for a place to buy.

W. W. M. D.

It's always hard to tell someone how to find your apartment when they all look so much alike. You can say, "Turn left at the concrete building after passing the concrete building that was past the first concrete building!" It was helpful when we had a junk car out in front of our apartment building, next to the street, beside the dumpsters. We could tell people, "Our apartment building is the one with the junk car out front." It was there for a year before someone took it away. Many times I would stare at the window and wonder to myself, "W.W.M.D.?" I don't have a bracelet for this, but I have asked myself, "What would Martha do?" Martha Stewart that is! When faced with a country as esthetically challenged as Ukraine, where would you start to try to get rid of the old Soviet look?

In the case of the junk car, I thought geraniums in the dashboard would be lovely. There was no windshield, so they could get plenty of rain and they'd look great all along the dash in a row. I didn't do this of course, but I should have! I thought that maybe when they were sentencing Martha to jail, they could have had her work out her sentence, like community service. She could have been sent to Ukraine to do a major makeover, but she only got six months and it would have had to have been a life sentence to have enough to get the job done! Even this famous, "do it yourself," guru," would have her skills challenged after what seventy years of communism has left behind.

You know the old saying, "Cleanliness is next to godliness." Well, I can sure see the opposite here; dirtiness and atheism! There are a few streets in the downtown area and a few other places that are kept clean, but the rest of the city is filthy. Every morning there is always new trash to be cleaned up. So many people won't take the time to throw it in their trash can indoors; they just toss it out the window or from their balcony. They figure the person that is in charge of the apartment grounds will clean it up; it's their job. So with all this litter everywhere and not much grass, it looks really dirty. Drainage is a problem in lots of places, so after it rains or the snow melts it's really a muddy mess in most neighborhoods.

You must always be careful walking close to the edge of buildings. You never know what might come flying out of the windows! I've almost been hit by flying hot cigarette butts and once a potato just missed me! My friend Stephanie was drenched by someone's wash tub full of yucky water! She was on her way to an appointment and got there sopping wet! I wonder why people don't pour it down their sink or tub? In the winter time you have to be really careful to stay away from the edge of buildings due to forming icicles. They can get really long and sharp. They break off and hit people and it's sometimes fatal. Many buildings downtown rope off the sidewalk where there is danger of this happening.

When you're outside walking on the sidewalk, you'd better watch out for other flying "stuff" because when men have a stuffy nose, they press one side of their nose with their finger and give it a good blow! But if you think about it, blowing it into a rag and putting it into your pocket is gross too, but at least you're not sharing it with the world! There's a lot of spitting going on also. Most of the time, they just spit right on the sidewalk. First you hear them, and then it lands in front or behind you.

Then there are the dogs, lots of dogs. There are lots of stray dogs too. I used to see this one guy walking his three huge dogs everyday. I don't know how he lived in such a small apartments with so many big dogs. When all the neighborhood dogs are walked, they leave presents every where, sometimes even on the sidewalk, so sometimes you've got to dodge these too. If you stray from the sidewalk at all, you're for sure to hit one of these doggy landmines. All throughout the day, I maneuver my way around all these germy things produced by man and beast. This obstacle course reminds me of why the tradition here, of not wearing your shoes indoors, is a **good** thing.

I can never seem to keep ahead of the dust in apartment, so I've given up! Every apartment we've lived in has been so dusty. It must be all the concrete walls and ceilings. It's like they're constantly molting or something! I vacuumed up a dust bunny behind the door the other day, and it was so big, it scared me! I thought it was a bunny! You know the joke about the kid hearing the verse saying we came from dust and to dust we'll return? And he asked his mom why there were so many dead people under his bed? That's what I think about every time I look under mine. I can dust one day and two days later you can write your name on the coffee table. Now, I don't mind if people write their names on the table as long as they don't write the date too!

Buying and Selling Apartments

Ukraine is one place you want to have a good realtor when you're involved in buying or selling property. We have always used the same one since we moved here and without her, there's no telling what kind of mess we would have gotten ourselves in to. When you buy or sell here, you meet all the parties involved at the bank or notary's office. The notaries are the most powerful people in town.

They can make or break your deal. Many times they will make it impossible for your deal to go through without bribing them. Most people must have bribe money in their budget, right along with rent and groceries! Bribing is part of the corruption that is a way of life here. They can make things very difficult for you just to make the extra money. I've been told notaries can make between $1000-$2000 a day! This is from taking advantage of people who are at their mercy. They can find all kinds of problems with your documents, or make up rules as they go. Praise God we didn't run into any problems during our closings.

You wouldn't believe the amount of money you have to pay now for these ghetto looking apartments. How could something made out of concrete cost so much and require so many documents? Well at least there was one document this massive chunk of concrete didn't require- a termite letter!

Since we were trying to sell our apartment, and knew we'd have to settle up any utility debts before we closed, we just quit paying the electric bill, since we weren't living there. They can't disconnect you because they'd have to turn off every apartment to do so. We had a weird situation with our meter anyway, so I just stopped paying. Since it took a year to sell the apartment, I was expecting to pay at least $250(the usual $20 or so a month).

I spent several hours getting this bill paid. I stood in line for two and a half hours, and then they closed the window for lunch! I was one person away from being waited on! After lunch, I gave the woman my info and told her, well Sanich told her, why I was there and that we hadn't paid in a long time. She looked on her computer at our account, got out her calculator and started scribbling stuff down on paper. I watched her toil over this for about twenty minutes, then she confidently handed me the bill. It was a whopping $12! I knew not to even try and ask her why. I had tried to settle things like this before. I was just glad to have the paper I needed to show that we were debt free to the electric company. Now I can understand why their government has a hard time making ends meet!

So we're sitting at the bank waiting to purchase an apartment, and we get all the paperwork done and it's time to pay. When I mean pay, I mean pay out the cash! Right then and there, you fork over **cash** for your apartment. People here do this every day. Even those who spend $500,000 or more on a home pay in cash. I haven't heard of anyone yet having this done electronically, bank to bank. It can be kind of nerve racking going to the bank to pick up this amount of money, then heading to another bank or notary's office with it. Then they lock you up in a room where each $100 dollar bill is fed through a machine to count it and check it to make sure it's not counterfeit.

During our first apartment purchase, when we handed over the cash to the owner, he asked Timmy, "Where did you get this money?" and Timmy replied, "I printed it this morning." Since counterfeiting is so bad in Ukraine, the seller didn't think Timmy's joke was that funny. I thought it was a great line! "What a witty husband I have," I thought. But the guy we were buying from kind of gave me the willies. It was as if I could hear music from the *Godfather* playing, so he probably wasn't the best guy to joke around with.

When we sold our old place, we had to wait forever at one bank for another bank to deliver the money for the buyers. We waited for several hours, then it finally arrived. I'd never seen or held this much cash before. It was wrapped up by the bank in bundles, but it was still counted by a machine again. We had to carry this money home with us on the subway, because our bank was already closed by the time we closed the deal! We figured carrying it on the metro was safer than a taxi. Suppose we got in a wreck and had tens of thousands of dollars flying out on the highway or taken from us while we injured or worse! So we felt fine crammed into the metro car with thousands of people and thousands of dollars in a backpack!

Buying a place and actually getting to move in it are two very different things. When we finally had closed the deal with this couple, we were to meet them at the apartment and pick up the keys. They had had months to get ready for the move. Well, I got there with my realtor and this family had **not even started** packing yet! It was a Friday, and we told them they could have until Monday to get out. The woman who lived there just laughed out loud in my face and said **she** wasn't getting out by Monday!

Her realtor was there also and made suggestions to where they could move while they were waiting on their new place to be available. There were places they could rent by the day or week, or how ever long they needed. This woman said, "I'm not moving into some one else's dirty apartment!" Oh! How I almost burst out laughing! I couldn't believe this woman dared to say such a thing, since she herself had not cleaned the apartment we were standing in, in the seventeen years she had lived there! I'm not kidding! The upstairs addition was only two years old, so why was the toilet black inside? Because I don't think it had been cleaned since they got it! My friend Laurie, what a friend, thought we could save it, so she cleaned it for me. It took **one hour** of hard scrubbing to get it white and shiny again! So you can see why we had to totally gut the downstairs to get the nastiness out.

They finally moved out about a month later, which really pushed us to get the remodeling done on schedule. If the tables had been turned, I'm sure they would have gotten the police and had us thrown out. During this time, they refused to pay anything for staying there either, so I was able to get some furniture that they wanted to sell me as payment, but believe me, they didn't want to do this either. I had to be firm and not let them continue to walk all over us.

Movin' on Up…to a Deluxe Apartment in the Sky…..

We finally got to move in. We now live on the top floor of an eighteen story apartment building. We also have a second floor, that's not listed in the elevator, which people on the top floor of some buildings can add to their apartment. The former owners had done this, so we have a two-story apartment. Shortly after moving in, I began to notice paint chips falling from the cracks, where the concrete slabs met, in the ceiling of the second floor. One morning, while it was still raining from the night before, I heard thumping sounds as I was coming up the stairs. Water was leaking through the cracks and there were puddles forming on our hardwood floors! I immediately mopped up and put down plastic.

It finally stopped raining and after the cracks dried, I caulked the cracks with silicon and taped plastic sheets on the ceiling. I would be ready for the next rain while trying to find out what the problem was. Of course I had to have an English speaking Ukrainian go with me to the building administrator's office to see about getting the roof fixed. We had to put our request or complaint in writing and then wait for a response. Well, I waited for about a month or so, but heard nothing; I wasn't surprised. But I was surprised when I contacted them, and they said they didn't have the money for this and if I wanted it fixed, I'd have to pay for it myself.! Of course this was absurd. Whoever heard of someone paying for a repair on the outside of their apartment building, plus we already pay a monthly maintenance fee! Of course all of our Ukrainian friends said not to pay it, but we had to or our second floor would be ruined. Well, I told them to send someone over to assess the situation.

The next day, two maintenance workers came over, looked at the roof and said it would take $350 to repair **our** fourth of the roof; about 600 square feet. There was no labor charge; they were already on salary for maintenance. I was pleased with this low estimate and agreed, but I had to pay up front, so they could buy the materials. I wasn't too comfortable with this. They weren't going to give me any agreement on paper or any receipt. They said I just had to trust them! I thought, "What idiot would agree to this?" Well, I was the idiot! I had no choice. I reluctantly forked over the money and asked God to please make these guys come back and do the work! The next day, my prayers were answered. The guys came back and did a great job! Thank you Lord!

Even though we own our place, it's still a lot different than living in a house. You just don't have the privacy or freedom that comes with a home. Many times I have an audience when I come home from the grocery store, especially in the summer. A lot of people are sitting out on the benches in front of the building entrance when I arrive with my driver and a car full of groceries. It is embarrassing having the ability to buy so much at one time. Even just a weeks worth of what an American buys looks like months worth to a Ukrainian. And then there's the loading of the elevator. By this time, I've handled my groceries more than I've wanted to. Picking them up, and then putting them down again. The floor of the elevator is not where you want your grocery bags to sit. I hate bringing these bags into my house and putting them down on my clean floor. I try to keep them in the entry way so not to spread the dirt and germs around.

What's a Thermostat?

The sooner they start privatizing more things around here the better. For example: the government still controls the heat. They turn your radiators on around October 15 and they're turned off on April 15. So the next time you're getting your tax returns in on the final day, think about what this date means for us and say a prayer that we won't have a lot of cold weather or snow in April! When our friends, Robbie and Criss McAlister had moved over in 1995, I would read their newsletter and feel so sorry for them when it was sooo cold, and their heat was either sooo bad or not on yet, they could see their breath inside their apartment! This warm weather lovin', southern girl didn't want any part of that! So when we rented our first place, I sure was hoping for good heat. We often have to pull out our space heaters before and after the turn on / turn off dates. One of our friend's children asked his mom what a thermostat was, since he'd grown up over here and had never seen or used one. Sometimes it's too hot with the radiators on, and we crack the windows; that's our thermostat!

I hate to see the radiators go off, because they really dry our clothes fast. They haven't had dryers for sale here until recent years, and I still don't really need one. We have a clothesline on our balcony and radiators for the winter. I've had my towels freeze on the balcony before. It's really weird to hold a frozen towel. You can knock on it and it's hard! Is this what you call, "freeze dried?"

Taking Things For Granted

How often do you thank the Lord for your utilities? If you're like me, you've always taken this for granted. It wasn't until I experienced life in another world that I even thought about it being a luxury. You know, it **is** a luxury? There are places in Ukraine that have never had hot water and their electricity is limited. Even in Kiev, we have disrupted services. In the early years, they would turn off the hot water during most of the summer. They said they were doing some kind of maintenance. It was hard having dirty, little kids, who after a hot and sweaty day, have to wait for their mom to boil them some water to mix in the tub with the cold. We called them bird baths and if you were good, you got a three potter instead of a shallow two! Over the years, the time that the water has been turned off has been gradually been reduced to only two weeks during the summer. After a few years of this inconvenience, and spilling boiling water on my foot, we decided to get an attachment for our shower head that heats up the water like a coffee maker. It was one of the wisest decisions we've made here.

There are other times that we don't have hot water. These are just random, maintenance times that are unannounced and usually several times a week. If someone is remodeling or needs their water cut off for a repair, then the whole building has to be cut off. These times can last from an hour to one or two days! It may be just the hot, or the cold or both. It's rare to have both gone for more than a day. It's a real pain when you're in the middle of preparing for twenty-five people coming over for supper and the water is turned off. I still drives me crazy when this happens. Picture this: It's early afternoon and you're up to your elbows in 150 chicken wings, and your water is turned off! There's no water to wash them or your hands in! Timmy had to go get some jugs of water from the neighborhood artesian wells, so I could finish preparing the meal. We have these wells in all the neighborhoods, because you're not supposed to drink the tap water that comes to your sink through the yucky old pipes of the building. Even the well water looks suspicious to me, so we drink bottled water. There's just something I like about drinking clear water!

Preparing food is one hassle when the water goes off, but I've heard of worse. How about the water going off when you're in the middle of coloring your hair, ladies? Do you stick your head in the toilet and use the one flush it has left, for that needed rinse, or let it burn? I've always kept an extra jug of tap water on hand, ever since I heard these kinds of stories!

The electricity hasn't been much of a problem, but we've had our moments. There was a time we were having power outages several times a week, for one to three hours a night. This went on for several weeks. The kids are trying to do their homework by candlelight, but there was stuff they need the computer for, but the desk top was out and the battery on the laptop only lasted for so long.

One night, shortly after moving to Kiev, we heard what looked and sounded like firecrackers coming from a small, concrete, utilities building in front of our apartment building. I could see out of the window that all the apartment lights in the neighborhood, including ours, were starting to blink and grow fainter. Then everything went black. With all the sparks we'd seen and the sounds we'd heard from that little building, I thought it would be months before we had electricity again, but to our amazement it was back on in thirty minutes. I was impressed and very thankful.

When you enter these old apartments, like ours, you can't help but notice all the bundles, or blobs, of wires that are exposed in the hallways, hanging above somewhere on the wall, at every apartment door. I don't think this is according to code! Or may I ask, "Is there a code?" If there is a code, it can be easily disregarded by a bribe somewhere down the line. It's pretty scary to think of Ukraine as one big fire hazard when you live here! Hey, at least everything is concrete; it may be smoking, but it'll still be standing! It's even scary for us when a light bulb blows out. When I say blows out, I mean blows up! They sometimes explode when you turn the light on. I usually let out a scream and everyone else knows what happened. Sometimes it trips the fuse box, and the whole apartment goes out. How many of you have to get out the vacuum cleaner and clean up, just because a light bulb burns out? I didn't think so.

You'll never see me replace a bulb with the light switched on, that's for sure. After the light has blown up or flown out the socket in part, it leaves the metal piece still screwed into the light. We then have to get that out, making sure the light is switched off, and then use some pliers to loosen it. This was a several times a week event at our other apartments, but where we are now it's only once in a while. The electricity is just weird here. At our present apartment, sometimes when the doorbell rings, my bed side lamp comes on! This used to happen at our old place too. For a while, I just thought I had left my light on or wondered who had left it on. But finally I was in the bed, in the dark and my light came on by itself when someone rang the bell. I finally had caught it in the act!

I've had friends who would be shocked while using their bathroom or kitchen sink, because there was current coming through the water some how! Talk about having your wires crossed! Now that's scary!

I was glad to get my dishwasher grounded, because I was scared when loading it. If my hands were wet, which they usually were, I'd get shocked if I touched the metal sides. So I had to be careful. The kids sure got out of a lot of dish work because of this. Also my microwave would give me some juice too, if I touched a certain spot on it with wet hands. I was glad when we moved and renovated the wiring. I now have a shock free kitchen!

So next time you're complaining about your high utility bills, let me remind you: you get what you pay for! Also you can see your tax dollars at work, more than I can say for here. They pay 65 % in taxes and don't get too much for it.

It Couldn't Get Anymore Awkward Than This!

There are other unusual things that make living in an apartment here very interesting. When someone passes away in the neighborhood, we get to have another cultural experience. They have the wake at their apartment, so you can easily see what's going on when it's time for the actual funeral. They bring the kitchen stools out to the entrance of the apartment to set the casket on, and they proceed with the service. If the family can afford a four piece brass band, you'll here them playing and see the family and friends walking in a procession to the funeral bus, and everyone rides together to the burial.

What's really bad about this is when I've been out shopping and have come home with my groceries and there is a funeral going on right in front of my door! It's very awkward to round the corner and suddenly see an open coffin in front of the only entrance to your apartment! The coffins are the shallow kind, shaped like the one Dracula hangs out in; with the dome lid to match. You can't help but see the person lying there, you don't have to look down in the coffin, they're right there! I usually just turn around and find some where else to hang out until they're done.

Usually we get a heads up on an upcoming funeral. One day Micah was coming in, and he told us that he just passed some men carrying out a big black bag(a body bag), or someone comes to the door collecting money for flowers for the funeral, so we know to look out for the funeral the next day.

So you can see why I might miss the privacy of a home and having a yard sometimes, but Timmy sure doesn't miss the maintenance! But apartment living in Kiev does put you right in the thick of things. There are hundreds of people in our building, so we have a lot more contact with people than if we were in a house. Also living on the eighteenth floor gives us more opportunity to meet a lot of them; we're always the last ones out of the elevator!

I Like It Anyway

For the most part, every neighborhood looks like an inner city ghetto. It has all the sights, sounds and smells that go along with the, "wrong side of the tracks," part of town.

In our first place, I used to look out the window and feel as if I had been sentenced to prison and the view from my seventh story kitchen window was a lovely view of the prison compound! That's exactly what it looked like and still does to this day, almost ten years later. Our friends Steve and Danelle, who are living in this same apartment right now, wouldn't contradict this. Thank goodness there are a lot of trees around to give it some color, especially in the fall; God's creation, adding beauty to the buildings created by atheists!

I like the winter too, especially the snow. It's a pure, beautiful blanket that makes things cleaner, at least for a little while. I'd have fresh snow every day of the winter if it was up to me. Being from the South, I've never experienced such snowy weather, so it's something different for a change. It also reminds me of verses that refer to things, ugly things like our sin, being made "As white as snow." It's **so** white! Snow really does make ugly things clean and beautiful. I have to laugh when I read Proverbs 31:21, which says, "When it snows, she has no fear for her household…" The Lord knew this South Carolina girl would be ok.

THE MISSIONARY PRAYER

When you're living in a different culture, you're going to come across some interesting foods that will be hard to stomach. During these inevitable moments, you pray the missionary prayer which is, "Lord, I'll get it down, if you'll keep it down!" Some of our experiences eating with Ukrainian families have come down to this prayer. Timmy was served a big hunk of this beautiful looking dish called, "shoeba." It looked like a big three layered cake with mayonnaise for the icing and chopped up boiled eggs for sprinkles! But it wasn't dessert! It consisted of fish, beets and who knows what else. I'm not too big on fish, and when they offered me a slice, I said I would just have some of Timmy's, since they had given him such a large piece.

Being the considerate wife I am, I let him dig in first. I could tell by his less than excited countenance, that he was thinking, "Wouldn't it be better to just tell them I don't like it, than to throw up at the table?" Both choices were rude, especially the latter, so he silently prayed the prayer that would hopefully keep this morsel of greasy fish cake in his stomach instead of it making a second appearance. I've found that bread makes a great chaser for these kinds of moments and praise God there's always bread at the table.

One of the most joked about treats among the missionaries is something called, "*sala*." In America we call it, "fatback." At the outdoor meat markets, you can see big pieces of it rolled up like quilt batting! Here, they eat raw pieces of this white, fatty stuff; I can feel their arteries clogging after every swallow! From where I come from, we cook our beans with it for flavoring, and then throw it out. Some people might eat a little piece fried, but not raw! I once, by mistake, bought some frozen dumplings to cook, bit into one, only to find out I had gotten the ones with sala in the center! Yum! Too bad I couldn't read the label.

Let me tell you about another little indulgence. When you're in the market, you can smell this snack long before getting to them; smoked prunes! I don't mind prunes so much; in fact, I think they get a bad rap. Smoked ones, on the other hand, I can't handle. They have them piled two feet high on the market tables. And some of the things they make with them are not natural; in fact, they should be against the law! My neighbor bought my son Micah a box of chocolate-covered, smoked prunes for his birthday! Talk about nasty! I tried one, and it took forever to get the charcoal like taste out of my mouth! I've always loved chocolate anything, but this crossed the line. They even make juice and ice cream with these smoky, dried up plums. That's just wrong!

They also sell these awful looking, head still on, dried fish. I can't eat something that is staring back at me! They say it's the treat of choice with beer. I wouldn't know, but I'm sure I'd have to drink enough beer first, so I wouldn't know what I was eating!

Europeans also put weird stuff on pizzas. Maybe they do this in the States and I've missed the Pizza Hut commercials advertising tuna as one of the toppings! I accidentally bought a frozen tuna topped pizza and it was disgusting! My cat wouldn't even eat it! And let's not forget some of the other toppings, corn and the fungi. Fungi has never been an attractive way to describe mushrooms, even though that's what it is, you don't want to see its real name on the pizza box or menu!

Ukraine and Russia are known for their caviar. I've had the unfortunate opportunity to eat this a few times and fortunately gotten out of others. The black variety is the pricey stuff, the orange eggs are cheaper. They usually spread some butter on a piece of bread and sprinkle these little orange, fishy beads on top of this. Yummy! They have caviar flavored snack food too.

You may have caviar served at a birthday party, wedding reception, and recently I heard of a new occasion, Sunday school! Our friends Jeff and Donna Crane, who moved here in 2007, were visiting a church with their family. When she went to pick up her kids from Sunday school, there her four year old was with a slice of bread and some lip-smacking, orange caviar on it! And she was eating it! It wouldn't take long for a church in America that decided to serve caviar, to lose their younger members to the church on the next corner that serves Little Debbie's during their Sunday school!

Overall, I'd say I like Ukrainian food as long as I don't have to eat every thing that's put in front of me. I went into this really nice Ukrainian cafeteria once to video all they had to offer, so I could show some of the dishes to a kid's Sunday school class that was featuring us as their missionaries. Well, it wasn't long before the manager game out and told me I had to stop filming. You would have thought I was a spy from CIA. He wouldn't give me any reasons why I wasn't allowed to film, he just made me stop. I had already gotten enough footage before he caught me though. But later, I heard about our friend Dai, the headmaster of our school, finding a roach in his borsch while eating there! Umm, maybe they thought I was filming for the restaurant inspectors, if there is such a thing here!

Ukrainians Meet Brownies (And more!)

I've loved feeding Ukrainians American food! I enjoy introducing new foods to our friends. It's fun to watch them try something they've never had before. They seem to like just about everything I've put in front of them except vegetables that are just served by themselves. They are just a little skeptical of a big bowl of corn or peas with nothing else mixed with it. They mix most of their vegetables together into some kind of salad, so it's weird for them to see a bowl of just one vegetable by itself on the table. Now they did like it when I served corn on the cob. I had found some frozen corn on the cob that was good and served it to a dining room full one night. They couldn't believe how "tasty" it was. (This is their favorite word to use.) Anyway, they went on and on about how good it was. Come to find out, that they boil their corn three hours when they're preparing it! Why? I have no clue! No wonder mine tastes better after only boiling it about twelve minutes.

They especially like American desserts; brownies are their favorite. I remember asking a Ukrainian if he'd like a brownie and he said, "Yes, what is it?" Many of their desserts aren't very rich, kind of like a cracker compared to a cookie. They do have lots of cookies I like, actually too many, but they seem to like our richer concoctions. Once we had a friend over, and he brought his mother for us to meet. For dessert, I served cheesecake from a cheapo, boxed, instant cheesecake mix that I had brought from America. While savoring every bite, she said, "I bet the Queen of England eats something like this." I decided then, that it doesn't take much to please my Ukrainian guests.

They can really hold their sweets too! I've never seen anyone eat so many sweets at one time. They have what they call a, "*slotski stol*," which means, "sweet table." So if you get invited to one of these, you've been invited to dessert. Whenever I serve cake, I've watched these skinny college students eat four slices with no problem. They can even eat two or three pieces of cheesecake; I almost get a stomachache watching them!

During Christmas, we love to have lots of parties and introduce our Ukrainian friends to some or our traditions and holiday foods. I can't always find what I need for some of these seasonal treats, but I manage to make a few things they've never had before; well really they've never had any of the things before. I had to stop a fellow from eating a peanut butter cookie that he had loaded with spinach dip! He didn't know what the cookie was; he thought it was just another cracker, just fatter.

I usually have to give instructions for meals, just in case they don't know what to do with something. I'm often hesitant to serve tossed salad with meals, because first of all, they don't use lettuce in a salad like we do (they usually just eat lettuce leaves by themselves). And secondly, they go crazy when using salad dressing! I realized early on that Ukrainians love sauces, sour cream and any other kind of condiment. They use a ton of it on whatever they are eating. I think I scared someone once when I yelled, "No, you're not supposed to do that!" I was witnessing someone pouring ranch dressing all over their whole plate of food! I still have to police the dressing when we're having salad.

Once in America we saw a food eating contest on TV, and there was a Ukrainian contestant; a skinny guy named Oleg. When they announced that the contestants were about to eat as much mayonnaise as possible, in a certain amount of time, we knew Oleg was going to win! The other contestants were all huge, American men. They strutted out acting very confident, but when the final bell rang, Oleg had won by eating eight pounds of mayo! We have this show recorded and enjoy showing it to our Ukrainian friends.

CHAPTER 10

THE MEDICAL WORLD

Tuberculosis, hepatitis, and AIDS are epidemics here. We've had people in our home who are under treatment for TB and others who might have one of the above unaware. It didn't take me long to figure out why some of this might be happening. During our summer visit, I saw something that really gave me a clue about how these germs might be spreading. We a missions team over, and our party was dining in a hotel restaurant waiting for a table. This hotel, which proudly displays its three stars next to its name, is in actuality, about a half-star establishment! Well, the waitress was in the middle of putting a fresh tablecloth on our table. The next thing I knew, she grabbed the pitcher of water from the table, filled her mouth straight from the pitcher, and then used her mouth as a sprayer to mist the tablecloth! She was trying to get the wrinkles out. She blew it all over; it sounded like a whale blowing through his air hole when he surfaces! So much for the "fresh" tablecloth; that hepatitis shot I got will be useful after all!

It's easy to see how things spread here because of some of their communal ways.

For example: some of the churches we've been involved in like to share a single cup with a hundred or more people when having communion! It's nothing personal, but I'd rather not do that!

If you happen to have a bottle of coke or something, then they think nothing of having some and passing it around. I don't even do this with my own family! You'll have them over for some coffee or tea, and it's nothing for someone to lick the spoon and return it to the sugar dish! I try to have serving spoons in everything, but many times they just help themselves with their own utensils. We have double dipping rules where I come from! And if the ketchup bottle has a few drips around the top, you just might see someone licking it off, thinking they're helping you out.

During the summer, usually at busy street corners, they sell a non-alcoholic, beer- like drink called *kavas*. I couldn't believe it when I saw people go up to this tank, pay the lady, drink a glass and then put the same glass down over a little fountain of trickling water for the next person to use. This went on all day. Who knows how many hundreds of people used this glass in a day or thousands by the time it was really washed! Years later they are finally using disposable cups. This method of just rinsing dishes and not washing them like we would, with a hot soapy dish rag, is quite common. I've had people visiting in my on home, get a drink of water or use a dish, rinse it off and put it right back in the cabinet. Many times, after having some of our Ukrainian friends house sit for us while we are in the States, I've had to wash dishes that were supposedly cleaned and were put back in the cabinets.

From what I hear, Ukrainian doctors love taking out appendixes, and they seem pretty good at it. Our friend Neva had a ruptured appendix and was taken by ambulance to the hospital. What a ride it was! She wasn't lying down on a gurney; she had to sit in a swivel, desk chair that was rolling around in the back of the ambulance and just hold on!

She got to the hospital, had the surgery and lived to tell about it. Praise the Lord!

As you can see, the ambulance service here is interesting. I can't imagine what kind of service they have in the rest of Ukraine if Kiev, the capital, has the best. One day, our friend Robbie answered his doorbell to find a woman standing there asking for his help. She wanted help with the neighbor in the next apartment. Robbie wondered what kind of help? Did she need some furniture moved or something? Well, he walked over to the other apartment to find a man lying on the floor from a stroke or heart attack. This woman was with the EMS, not that she had a uniform or anything, and needed Robbie to help her put this man on the gurney. You may be wondering why this woman was by herself? Well, the ambulance driver was sitting in the ambulance; that's his job. He wasn't going to leave the ambulance to help her, even though she could have used a hand. This was awhile back; hopefully they have three people in the ambulance by now.

Timmy had just started some cholesterol medicine when we moved over, and so after a few months, he had to have some blood work done. He went to one of the better clinics in town, and had his blood checked and to his surprise, they told him he didn't have high cholesterol! Wow! The medicine must have really worked a miracle! No, not really. We're not sure what they were talking about with their test results, but we think Timmy's cholesterol numbers translated into some other scale that obviously gave us a false diagnosis.

When Steve and Danelle were having trouble with their cats, the vet came over many times and treated the cats, but he also treated them! When they mentioned they (not the cats) had a rash, he was very upset and they hadn't told him sooner. He took them in the bathroom, turned the light off and shined a blue light on their rashy skin to see what kind of rash it was. He was very concerned that their teenage daughters, Merry and Grace would become sterile because of this rash they had gotten from the cats! He was relieved to see it wasn't the rash he was worried about. We've laughed with our friends about this possible rash of sterility, but also because they're the only **people** I know who have been treated by a vet!

Ukrainians, especially the older generation, love to sit in saunas. When given the opportunity, I've always turned it down. I was born and raised in a sauna (South Carolina summers), so why would I purposely sit in a hot, sweltering room to sweat! They're telling me how healthy it is; all the while they've got vodka in one hand and a cigarette in the other! The life expectancy for men here is about fifty-eight, so until that rises, I'll probably stick to what I know.

February seems to be, "National Flu Month," around here! All the schools usually close down for the month because of what they call, "*Grip.*" There are quarantines in the hospitals, college dorms, and so on. It's a tradition. You can tell it's official when you see the clerks in the stores wearing their surgical masks. I hate to get out in the crowds during this time, but Ukrainians believe you should go outside **every** day. I don't know if this is for health reasons or this is a superstition. When we have really cold weather, you still see people out strolling with their babies, heading somewhere in these heavy duty strollers that look like they have four-wheel drive. The babies are so wrapped up with clothes and blankets, they've never known they left their room!

In South Carolina, you wouldn't see someone out of the house in snowy, single degree weather, especially pushing a stroller! We've actually had weather like this twice in S.C. and believe me, you don't go out unless you need something desperately. But you usually in the South you get everything you need, along with everyone else that storms the grocery store two days before, when you heard snow **might** be on its way! Ukrainians laugh when I tell them how the southerners, bless our hearts, go wipe out the stores of all the milk and bread when we have the threat of winter weather. And they really get a kick out of how our schools close when it starts to snow. Here, they don't close the schools unless the classroom temperature drops to 15 degrees!

The kids here are dressed for the winter even when it's spring. If you don't have your kids dressed warm enough, you will be harassed by many a babushka until you have every inch of the child's flesh covered, especially the head! I feel so sorry for these screaming babies. Their faces are all red, their burning up from clothing overkill and their parents think it's the healthy way to go. I've even been outside on a breezy day, without a jacket and been stopped and fussed at by one of these ladies. I think all these babushkas were KGB officer's way back when, since they know everyone's business or try to make it their business.

From what I hear, the dentistry here is pretty good. Besides the few horror stories I've heard from a couple of Ukrainians, who had the wrong teeth pulled out, it sounds like you can find a good dentist; at least that's what my fellow missionary friends tell me. I still get my dental work done in America when we visit, since we have dental insurance. No need to take a chance on literally, "losing something in the translation!"

They do have some very nice offices with high tech equipment. I went in one once to get my daughter an x-ray for some orthodontic work. Yes, they also have good orthodontists here and for a fraction of the cost. The orthodontist I went to didn't do x-rays at his office, so we had to go to another part of town to a particular dentist to get this done. It was a very swanky place, and the prices were more like America.

Now the hours these professionals keep are bizarre, but quite convenient for a lot of people. Many are open long hours, seven days a week. My daughter had an orthodontist appointment on a Sunday morning and had to return later in the afternoon to have something else done. It is strange passing these offices at 9:00 at night and seeing people sitting in the chairs getting worked on.

Years ago, when you went to the doctor, even in some of the nicer places, you didn't get a hospital gown, when you really should have one on! You just are sitting or standing there, sometimes with doors open to hallways, with nothing on! Kind of drafty, especially in the winter! I've heard stories of people walking down hallways and seeing people just sitting around buck naked! I once had a chest x-ray and just stood around in this huge room with all these nurses and techs, with nothing on above the waist. I was cold and felt a little, "out there!" When I finally found this hospital, I was weary about going in any way. The building looked so dilapidated; I wondered how in the world could there be an x-ray machine in this place that was still working! I couldn't believe when I entered the room and saw this brand new Siemens machine! How did it get there? I didn't know God's guardian angels were into delivering high tech equipment just when I needed it!

My Foot: The Continuing Saga

I had had foot surgery in the States and after six weeks, returned to Kiev. After a few months of pain, thinking it was still healing, I decided to get an x-ray to see what was going on. I went to my neighborhood clinic, with someone who could translate for me. I entered into an old building that was dingy and dimly lit. I gave them my passport for information and sat to be waited on. It wasn't too long before I was greeted by the x-ray technician who was a little more cheerful and talkative than most. I didn't have to smell her breath to realize that she had had a little more than corn flakes for breakfast! I did remind her I'd like the lead apron if it wasn't too much trouble. Hey, I was surprised they had an apron! If you had been there with me, I would have given you the official Ukrainian, "Yep, thy're drunk," sign, by thumping the side of my neck.

The tipsy tech did offer me some medical advice though. She told me to make a paste of sour cream and salt, rub this on my foot, then cover my foot in cabbage leaves and sleep with it like this overnight. I smiled and thought about waking up with this, putting my foot between two slices of bread and I'd have lunch!

While sitting there, I took a good look around at the former Soviet clinic, but it seemed more like a current Soviet clinic! I didn't see anything that said otherwise. If I had looked hard enough through the pile of x-rays that were in disarray all over the small room, I probably could have found ones belonging to Lenin and Stalin! They had an unusual filing system; some on the floor, some on the table and a big stack on a chair.

The x-ray machine looked as if it may have been the first one ever off the assembly line. Even though it was an old machine and probably radiating more than my foot, it did produce a clear enough picture; a great picture of my broken foot! One of the bones they had worked on during my surgery was now broken. I had walked around several months with a broken foot! This tells you a little about my pain threshold, too high for my own good!

My surgery ended up doing me a lot more harm than good. My Ukrainian friends couldn't understand why I went all the way to America and paid thousands of dollars to get my foot messed up, when I could have gotten it messed up in Ukraine for whole lot less! At this point, I was beginning to wonder this myself!

This was my worse nightmare come true! A broken foot, in Ukraine, in the middle of winter! Crutches in the snow weren't exactly my idea of a good time. Now I had to decide how and where to get a cast put on. This clinic wasn't my first choice, and I'm not sure they even did casting, so I called my friend Sveta, that had worked at an American- type medical clinic. This nicer clinic had American prices too, but she knew the doctor that came in to do their casting and arranged for me to go to this doctor somewhere else and pay a lot less directly to the doctor.

We went later that night to a children's trauma hospital. It was traumatizing alright! The building looked like most buildings here, as if it should have a condemned notice tacked to the front door. Inside, we went looking for Dr. Katya. I saw a young woman in a dingy, stained, white coat cleaning the floor. She looked up at us and introduced herself; she was the doc I was looking for! I thought she was the cleaning lady! At that time, in 2004, working for the government-run hospital, she didn't make much more than a cleaning lady, only about fifty dollars a month and whatever she could make on the side from people like me. There's not quite the prestige in being a doctor as in America; they don't even get Dr. in front of their name.

It wasn't what I was used to, but I didn't have to fill out a thing. I loved that part! It didn't matter who I was, since I wasn't Ukrainian, there was no record keeping. She took me down the same kind of dimly lit hall as the previous place and into another very dimly lit room. The forty watt seems to be the bulb of choice in most buildings. She looked at the x-ray and began to ask me what kind of cast I preferred. I could have the cheap, plaster version or the scotch cast stuff that comes on a roll, goes on easy and quickly hardens. I chose the latter; the only catch was that I had to buy it myself! They didn't keep the expensive stuff on hand. So my dear, full-service, interpreter friend went to the nearby pharmacy and purchased the necessary goods. It was a whopping eighteen bucks! Which is whopping, compared to the few dollar plaster version. But my foot was worth it!

The doc did a great job on my cast. After slipping her twenty-five dollars, which was off the record, seeing there was no record for it to be off of any way, I was on my way. Wow! What a cheap ordeal. I should have gone all out and taken an ambulance home instead of a taxi! But would they have had a swivel chair for Sveta too?

On another cold, wintry day I went downtown to the main orthopedic hospital to get another x-ray. My stateside doctor wanted me to get one that showed another angle, to see if it was healing ok. I thought I had been upgraded from the little clinic, but this hospital was just a bigger version with a lot more people waiting in line. Well, when I was entering the hospital, I couldn't believe, well I could believe, how bad the sidewalks were. They hadn't been cleared of the snow and ice. There's nothing like trying to enter an orthopedic hospital, which has an entrance like a skating rink, while on crutches! I think they were producing their business right out front! This is only one example of how you can tell that Ukrainians aren't too worried about being sued.

After three months of hobbling around on crutches, through the snow and down icy paths, it was finally time to get my cast off. So back to Dr. Katya I went. This was another one of those times that I thought, "If only my friends could see me now!" She x-rayed it and it was good to go. I had already been wondering. Ok, that's a lie! I was **worrying** how she was going to cut the cast off. She then began to pull out all kinds of interesting tools; old, corroded, rusty tools! I thought, "Oh! This is where that tetanus shot I got years back comes in handy." She started in on the cast, a little cutting, a little sawing, and then back to cutting. These tools were about to break skin, the very skin I was about to jump out of! Finally after all the twisting, prying, and pulling, the cast was finally off. I paid her another twenty-five dollars. Again, you get what you pay for.

Whenever I have doctor appointments in the States now, I try not to ever complain about waiting or anything else that I hear most people complain about in the waiting rooms. Boy! They have no idea! So I share some of these stories with people who strike up conversations with me as we're waiting. Hopefully after our little chats, they're a little more thankful for the healthcare they've impatiently been waiting for.

CHAPTER 11

SOME THINGS I LOVE ABOUT UKRAINE

I love how your birthday isn't just one day. You can still get flowers a week later! And they don't just say, "Happy Birthday!" They toast you with all kinds of well wishes and blessings.

I love being able to share my beautiful southern accent with people who want to learn English.

I love the way Ukrainians love the simple things and simple pleasures.

I love when you're invited over, you're never rushed to leave.

I love how they have lots of trees in the city.

I love watching deaf people on the subway signing away in conversation.

I love how Ukrainians value togetherness around the dinner table. If there is more than one table, then you put them together, and you don't start until everyone is there.

I love being able to shop on the way home without entering a store and buying fresh produce on the sidewalk from a babushka's garden.

I love the snow.

I love how their lives don't revolve around three meals a day; they eat to live, not live to eat.

I love hearing accordion music echoing in the subway station.

I love Ukrainian ice cream and chocolate

I love the firework displays throughout the weekend for weddings, especially the ones that explode into red heart shapes!

I love being greeted by the stray cats on my walk to the grocery store.

I love getting medicine without a prescription.

I love that you don't have to have a car.

I love Ukrainian bread and borsch.

I love the way they say more than one, "yes," "Da,da,da,da,da."

I love being able to buy flowers from anywhere at such great prices.

I love all the new, big grocery stores.

I love the spring when all the chestnut trees are in bloom and the fall with all its yellow leaves.

I love the Crimean coastline: God's awesome creation

And most of all I love: the Ukrainian people, who have welcomed us and shared their lives with us and let us with them.

PART 2

A SERIOUS MISSION

When we started praying about moving to Ukraine, the Lord showed us these verses which seemed to be talking about Ukraine and what we were to do there.

Isaiah 61:1-6 (NIV)

The Spirit of the Sovereign LORD is on me, because the LORD has anointed me to preach good news to the poor. He has sent me to bind up the brokenhearted, to proclaim freedom for the captives and release from darkness for the prisoners, to proclaim the year of the LORD's favor and the day of vengeance of our God, to comfort all who mourn, and provide for those who grieve in Zion— to bestow on them a crown of beauty instead of ashes, the oil of gladness instead of mourning, and a garment of praise instead of a spirit of despair. They will be called oaks of righteousness, a planting of the LORD for the display of his splendor.

They will rebuild the ancient ruins and restore the places long devastated; they will renew the ruined cities that have been devastated for generations. Aliens will shepherd your flocks; foreigners will work your fields and vineyards. And you will be called priests of the LORD, you will be named ministers of our God. You will feed on the wealth of nations, and in their riches you will boast.

CHAPTER 12

THE EVILS OF COMMUNISM

I can't begin to do this subject justice. I can only give you a taste of what I've seen as the results of communism. I've already shared some funny and unusual cultural differences which may have resulted from communism, but the legacy of communism is an enormous tragedy that can't be made light of. There are many books describing the horrors of life, during this era, in this part of the world, so I don't need to write another one, but I do want to give you just a little glimpse of what we've learned while living in a post soviet country.

One of the communism trademarks is attempting to make everyone the same. Not only is it wrong, it just doesn't work. That's what separates true democracy from the rest. You can't make people the same. People are different in looks, aptitude, abilities, etc. In America, if you work hard, you get more. Taking initiative and leadership pays off.

During the decades of communism, there was no need to try and better yourself because your circumstances wouldn't change. You were just like everyone else, so why take initiative in anything. You couldn't really change your circumstances because you had no say so or control of your future. Why work harder or be smarter; it made no difference. Communism is such an abusive way of governing, both to the body and soul. After living here, I have a pretty good idea of what's going on in Cuba, North Korea, and China; it's not good. It strips people of dignity and their God-given potential. And what a mess you're left with when the government collapses!

The communists kept such a strong hold on the people in all walks of their lives. This control killed any creativity anyone had, since they had no right to use it. Since taking initiative could have gotten you killed back then, the country is still suffering today because of this. Now I think the fear of long ago has turned into apathy and laziness, or maybe they don't even realize this mentality has possibly been inbred in them. It's been so hard to find young men who will be leaders. They haven't been leaders in other areas in society, therefore this has overflowed into the life of the church and its lack of leaders.

During communism, you couldn't really stand up for your beliefs. Your beliefs had to be the same as the government or else you suffered the consequences. I think because of this, people have become non-initiators. Also the government did everything for you, and not in a quality way either. In return, you just did what they said, and you depend on them for everything.

Communism has to be the dullest way of governing a country. It has to be dull, that's part of the philosophy. When not acknowledging God's existence is the basis for your government, then your world has no other possibility than to be dull! Part of the oppression is this dullness: blah and ugly. Besides the older, historical buildings downtown and in the pre-communism era, most of the buildings are gray concrete. Every where you look, it's the same color. This look is evident throughout Europe wherever communism ruled. You can immediately see the communist part of Hungary, Poland, and other countries when you're there or just flying over.

I have heard it said, when you leave America or any Western Europe countries, and enter a country of the (FSU) Former Soviet Union; it's like going from a color TV to a black and white. This describes it exactly. The drabness here was part of the control of the communist. The lack of color is such a picture of hopelessness. Since independence, the newer buildings are bringing color and life into the décor of the city.

God is so unbelievably different than Communism; He's the exact opposite! That's why it's a joy to be here and share this difference with the Ukrainian people. Timmy met a guy in the park, who spoke English, and struck up a conversation with him. This man said during communism, when they were being told day after day there is no God, he knew deep down that there was, but there wasn't anyone who could tell him how he could know Him. Timmy was able to share the Gospel with this man and he received Christ. The second year we were here, even with my pitiful Russian skills, I tried to share with a woman in my building. With a great Bible that had English on one side the page and the same verses in

Russian on the other half, I began to talk to my new friend about God. She said, "God has forgotten about Ukraine." This broke my heart. I begin to tell her that He hadn't forgotten them, and that's why I had come! God showed me once again that what I was doing in Ukraine was so needed.

There is nothing like telling someone about God's love for them when they've never believed in God. Where do you even begin to tell someone about Christ dying for their sins when they've never even heard the Christmas story from the Bible before? I think that has been the most exciting thing here, being the first ones to tell the other side of the story to those raised in an atheistic world. We work a lot with the younger generation, who have mostly grown up since Ukraine's independence. However, they still were raised by their families, who were brought up during communism, so we still have to deal with this as major part of their foundation.

We can't begin to imagine what this nation has gone through. People were starved to death by their own government. The Nazis did even more horrible things. One day we were coming back from an outing with our friend Sanich, and he asked us if we wanted to drive back into the woods to where a, "killing field," was. The entrance to this forest was marked along the highway with the large metal crosses. I knew what it was, but had no idea what was in the woods. We drove down a shady, paved road that went into a forest of pine trees. When we got to the end, there stood a monument in memory of the tens of thousands and maybe hundreds of thousands of people who had been executed, murdered by their own government. For a long time, the Ukrainians had been told that this mass grave was the result of the Nazi occupation, but later it was revealed otherwise.

We got out of the car and I smelled an odor that I have never smelled before. It was a peculiar smell. As we looked around, there were many freshly dug pits with large bags beside them. There were two men there, security men, who were keeping watch over the weekend. We asked them what was going on out there. We were told that there was some excavating going on to try and identify some people from other countries, such as Poland and maybe they'd move some of these remains back to their homelands.

They told us the bags at each pit were full of people's bones. I couldn't believe it. I was glad I hadn't looked in one of the bags out of curiosity. Could this be what smelled, after so many decades? They continued to tell us that there were a lot more people buried in the woods than they had originally thought; that in each pit, they were so many bones layered on top of one another, they couldn't really tell who was who. They thought it was going to be impossible to try and identify any certain group of people. And to think, there are many, many more forest just like this one all over the country.

This forest was one of the eeriest places I've ever been and by far the saddest. There were ribbons tied to all the trees, and some had pictures of loved ones nailed to them by family members who knew their relatives had been executed and buried there. One tree had a picture of a young woman on it, a school teacher, who had been accused of being against the communist government, so she was killed. It was written also, that she was cleared of this accusation forty years later. A lot of good it did her.

I'm sure there were many believers among the executed, because a Christian was automatically considered a threat to an atheistic government. We've had opportunity to meet and know people here who have suffered greatly because of their Christian faith. One friend told us he remembers as a young man, how they would be meeting in the woods for church and get caught and the whole group would be arrested. They also would sneak out of the city during the night, travel two hours away to a lake where they could secretly have a baptism.

And to think, there are more people being martyred today than any other time. We can't relate to this kind of suffering, but our day may come. Right now, Ukraine has the freedom to spread The Gospel, and we pray this continues for many years to come, but Satan is regaining lost ground in Russia, Belarus, and many other former soviet countries.

He doesn't like what's going on and continues to use wicked leaders to have his way. Pray for this part of the world, especially for Ukraine. Pray that God will use the Ukrainians to reach all of its neighbors of the F.S.U., and that they will see themselves as missionaries; a vital force in reaching Eastern Europe for Christ.

CHAPTER 13

THE VALUE OF LIFE

When you take God out of the picture, you take the value of life out of the picture.

When we moved to the Ukraine in 1998 one statistic said the abortion rate averaged six abortions per woman! Can you imagine? This rate has dropped a some over the years with more ministries assisting in getting proper information out to help these women understand the damage abortions causes their bodies and what God says about destroying life. A medical student friend in our building interning as an obstetrician asked us one day about pregnant women expecting deformed babies … what is the responsibility of the parent and the doctor? She asked us, wasn't it her duty as a doctor to encourage these parents to have abortions, so they wouldn't have to deal with the stressful circumstances associated with handicapped and deformed children? It was a great opportunity to share with her God's prospective. We have been honored with many opportunities just like this one to share the truths of God's Word. We find that we must begin with the elementary lessons to help bring these folk not only to the realization of God's truths, but of the most basic knowledge about the sanctity of life and care giving.

One morning looking out my kitchen window I noticed an older man sitting on the bench in front of our entrance. His hat was hung over his face and his arm was draped over the back of the bench as if he was taking a nap. I had never seen him before, but I could tell something was wrong as I noticed his color was ashen. It was 8:00 and people were walking by on their way to work; some would stare, but most didn't seem too concerned. It's not at all uncommon to see drunks sitting or passed out on the ground or sidewalk. Sometime later I noticed policemen had stopped and seemed to be writing up a report. I then realized that the man had died.

The policemen never touched him; they just took their notes and left. At least two hours passed, when I saw a uniformed woman, with a black bag over her shoulder, who I assumed was the coroner. She move toward the body and gently picked the mans hands up to finger print him. A crowd never formed, no one seemed disturbed over this. There was no crime scene tape, and no one was questioned. This woman did her job, and left.

The whole day had passed and still this man was still sitting there, and people continued their regular routines around the body. Finally, around 8:00 PM his body was finally taken away. How sad that his life meant so little. The body was there for more than twelve hours. Did anyone miss him? Were they searching for him? We learned later that he actually lived in an apartment building right behind ours and that he had no living family. Generally when someone dies their funeral is held outside of the apartment the very next day. In this case, we didn't see or hear anything. I was struck by sadness to think about any person dying and no one caring.

Widows and the Elderly

Religion that God our Father accepts as pure and flawless is this: to look after orphans and widows in their distress... James 1:27 (NIV)

A dear 86 year old lady that I befriended our first year in Ukraine was a beggar who stood on our corner with her hand out waiting for money to come her way. Scenes like this one are common in Ukraine. Vera was her name which means "faith." Her age amazed me. I gave her money several times and was able to build a relationship with her over several months. She would hug me on the street as others looked on. Her head would fit snuggly in my chest. I thought she was so precious. I know others passing by were wondering why I was hugging such a person. When a translator was with me, I had the opportunity to share with her what I was doing in Ukraine, and then she told me her story. When she was a young woman, she had had an abortion. Can you imagine having this done 70 years ago in the Soviet Union? With tears streaming down her cheeks, she told of her terrible life and that God didn't have a place in heaven for her; that He couldn't forgive her. My heart was moved with compassion by her story and I was privileged to tell her that Christ had died for her sins. It wasn't our works that counted, but the work Christ had done for us.

When I invited her into our apartment for lunch I'm sure those watching thought I was crazy when they saw me walking home with the neighborhood beggar woman. What was this American doing? Why was she showing this woman any attention? Why would she care? My hope was that they saw Christ caring for her, through me. I wanted my believing translator to see this, too. It was important to show her how Ukrainian believers have many opportunities to express how Christ loves the ones we consider unloved.

I had prepared a soft, Ukrainian lunch for her, since she only had one tooth left. It dangled on her bottom gum when she would talk. I thought she had a beautiful smile! During lunch, we shared with her how much God loved her and all she had to do was give her life to Christ, and she'd have forgiveness of sin. After about two hours, of talking and sharing scripture, I think Vera understood for the first time that it wasn't through works that one has a relationship with God.

Later, as weeks passed, I didn't see her standing in her usual spot. I had been to her one room apartment once before when I had bought her some groceries, so I knew where she lived. It was the worse building on our street. I had known someone else that had lived in this building, and they had killed 20 mice in their one room apartment in one week! She didn't have much stuff. I noticed a McDonald's paper cup and a few other things she had gotten out of the trash.

She didn't have a phone, so I would have to try and find her at home. As the months went by, I knew in my heart that something had happened to Vera, and I didn't want to find out what I already knew. This little old lady, with a failing heart, was probably gone. So many times I had wanted to interview her, with a translator, and hear her life story and write it down. She had witnessed and lived through so much in her eighty-six years. I failed at this opportunity.

I finally was walking past her building one day and had a Ukrainian with me, so I decided to stop. When I got to her floor, and we asked a neighbor where Vera was; they told us she had died. I immediately started crying. I had missed being with her when she died; she had died all alone. People that cleared out her apartment probably wondered who I was when they found a picture of Vera and me that I had taken and given her. I know God gave Vera her long life just so she would be standing on my street corner when I moved to Ukraine and we'd have the time talk about Him and how she could be forgiven. I don't think she died alone after all.

There are many others like Vera in Ukraine. Never have I seen so many widows. What a ministry to widows people can have! I pass them on the street every day, and many of them live in my building. One night Timmy came in and told me there was an old woman kneeling in the snow, begging on the bridge near our metro stop. It was freezing cold, and I couldn't stand the thought of this poor woman out there, so I immediately took her some food and money. Hopefully she quit for the night and went home and got warm. Sometimes I'll give a begging babushka a Ukrainian bill that is worth about 20 cents or tell one of them, when I'm buying produce, to keep the change, and they kiss my hand, bless me, and go on and on thanking me with tears in their eyes.

These Babushkas have been the hardest hit over the years. They really struggle to make ends meet. Whenever I look out my kitchen window in the morning, I see these ladies coming to sell; struggling to cross the street with their loads. They look like a caravan of loaded down mules. They pull little wheeled carts and carry heavy bags on their shoulders; some of them, so humped over from this strenuous work, walk bent over, almost in half. Many bring their garden vegetables to town and sell them on the sidewalk. You see them in every neighborhood. Sometimes in the summer, there can be close to 100 women lined up near my apartment selling just strawberries.

They lost all their savings, like everyone else, when the communist government collapsed, and they get very little pension. It breaks my heart to see them begging for money or selling cigarettes in the subway station at 10:30 at night just to get by. If I'm ever out this late, I'm usually tired when I pass them standing there, so I can only imagine how tired they must be. Can you envision your mother or grandmother having to do this to survive?

Many times I think these ladies are a lot older than they are. Once I was with a friend and her mother. She told me it was her mom's birthday. I assumed her mother was at least in her sixties, but that even seemed too young, since she walked with a cane. I'm glad she didn't have me guess how old she was, because I would have really missed it. When she told me her mom was forty-nine, I tried not to act totally shocked! They always think I'm younger than I say; I'm sure my soft life has kept me from aging compared to the hardships they have endured. They've worked hard their whole lives, but communism never gave them a better, more comfortable life. Now communism is gone, and their youth is spent, but there were **never** any dreams of a pampered retirement anyway.

Orphans

Another great ministry here, that people can give themselves to, involves orphans. There are thousands of children in orphanages; from birth to teens. The sad thing is that most of these children aren't orphans. Either they aren't being cared for by their parents and are taken away because of neglect, or the parents themselves give them up, because they know they can't take care of them. Some parents dump their kids at an orphanage just because they were born with a crossed eye or they wet the bed or for other trivial reasons. It is sad when you're an unwanted or uncared for child and go into a system that gives you little hope for the future, in a country that views you as a second rate citizen.

There have been times when I've been approached by children on the street, who probably ran away from an orphanage, and are begging for money. They will follow you, tug on your shirt until you acknowledge them in some way. I usually don't give these kids any money, because they may spend it on glue for sniffing. I hate to see children doing this, and walking down the sidewalk, out of their minds. I try to buy them food instead.

One day I was in McDonald's eating lunch, when I noticed some pitiful, young boys going from one abandoned table to another, eating the scraps people had left on their trays. I couldn't stand watching this, so I went up to the boys and asked them if they wanted some food. They didn't hesitate to say yes. I bought them the works and enjoyed watching them eat. One of the four boys spoke a little English. I told them that Jesus was buying this food for them. I knew I had only helped them out for one meal, for one day. It was only a band-aid covering a much deeper wound than what I was seeing.

Another day, I was leaving a restaurant and a street kid asked for my leftovers that I was carrying from my meal I hadn't finished. Of course I gave it to him. I felt so sad that he was living such a dreadful life. There are ministries that deal with street kids, but it seems like there is a never ending supply coming from the orphanages.

Here are some statistics I read:
• There are over 100,000 orphans in Ukraine.
• Only 10% of orphans are in orphanages because of death of a parent, 90% are social orphans due to alcoholism, abandonment, or imprisonment of parents.
• There are 450 orphanages or orphan homes in Ukraine. Of these: 50 are baby houses 100 are regular orphanages for ages 8-17 100 are boarding schools for specialized needs including learning disabilities 100 are shelters where 30,000 children live temporarily between leaving home and being assigned to an orphanage.100 are private institutions, housing a total of 1000 children, mostly Christian efforts.
• There are presently 6,000 adoptions a year (almost all foreigners adopting).
• The older an orphan gets, the chances for his/her adoption drastically decrease.
¤ Each year many orphans between 15 to 18-years-old leave the orphanages.
• Most of these orphans have no one to turn to for help.
• 10% of them will commit suicide after leaving the orphanage before their eighteenth birthday.
• 60% of the girls will end up in prostitution
• 70% of the boys will enter a life of crime
• Only 27% of these youth will find work

Five teenage orphans explaining how they ended up in the orphanage:

"I don't remember my parents at all. When I was three, I was found at the train station. From there I was taken to the orphanage."

"My parents drank a lot. My mom died when I was 16. I don't know where my dad is. I've been in the orphanage system since I was four because my parents drank."

"I am from a big family; my parents couldn't feed us all. My dad died when I was five years old. After that my mom started drinking even worse, but I was already in the orphanage. I've lived there since I was two years old."

"My dad was put in prison when I was little. Mom started drinking. She drank so much that everything went towards her vodka, there was nothing to eat, nothing for us kids. When I was eleven, someone came and took all us kids to the orphanage."

"My mother died of a brain tumor when I was three years old. I never had a father really. They sent me to the orphanage when I was three."

We recently met a man in our building that was raised in an orphanage. He is twenty-eight years old now. He came over to a get together we had at our place. He stayed a little longer and told us some of his story. His parents were alcoholics and couldn't take care of him and his sister, so his grandmother kept his sister and put him in the orphanage when he was two. His parents eventually died in a fire. He was almost adopted by an American family when he was twelve, but it wasn't ever approved. He still treasures the letters he received from this family. He said he wanted to be part of a family so bad. This family has still kept in touch with him for fifteen years. His dream is to visit them in America someday, if he can get a visa. All these years later, he just met an aunt for the first time, and he and his sister don't get along, so still doesn't know what it's like to have family.

He said he became a Christian when he was about fifteen through a camp that some missionaries put on. We were excited to hear this and hope to become friends and fellowship together. His story broke my heart. Maybe in some way we can be a family for him. These stories are bad, but I've heard of even worse situations that some children have gone through before they got to the orphanage; horrific things that hopefully many were too young, and they won't remember what happened to them or their parents.

We have friends who specialize in taking in teenage orphans and preparing them for adulthood. They are housed and taken care of, trained in life skills and most importantly, given a chance to know Christ. They have to leave the orphanage when they are sixteen, then they're on their own, which usually ends up with them living on the streets. I really admire the foreign missionaries and Ukrainians that have taken these teens in to share God's love and hope with them. Hopefully many of these orphans will come to know Christ and experience their Heavenly Father's unconditional love as adopted sons and daughters.

CHAPTER 14

THE OVERWHELMING NEEDS

There have been many things to find humor in, in cross-cultural living over the years, but too many things still remain that could never be funny. I've tried to laugh when appropriate, but have wanted to cry many times over. The suffering I've seen here has been overwhelming at times, and I've felt like there is no way I could even begin to make a difference. It's easy to want to give up, but I know God can do the impossible, even if it's only one heart at a time.

There are so many physical needs among our friends and they're not the really destitute who live among us. I remember reading a statistic back in 2005 that said that 97% of Ukrainians lived at poverty or below. I know they live better than those in Haiti and some other countries, so I can't imagine being a missionary where it's worse off than Ukraine. We live in Kiev where it's much better off than other parts of the country. Still, the needs can be overwhelming, and the desire to help everyone is there, but it's impossible. We do what we can, but we have to discern who to help and who not to.

Sometimes it's easy to know when it's the right time to help someone. Once I was with a dear Ukrainian friend shopping in the outside market. It was a cold winter day, and we were walking around in slushy, melting snow. I had on warm boots, but my friend made a comment about her feet being wet and cold because her boots were torn and she could feel water in her shoes as we walking around. I knew she didn't have money for new boots, so I stopped right then and told her I wanted to get her some new boots there in the market. I couldn't let her continue to walk around with cold, wet feet. I wouldn't take no for an answer; it was the right thing to do.

So many times we want to help people, but want to do it anonymously. In the States, we could do this very easily, but it's much more difficult here. If we do something like give money or buy someone a new coat, people always know it's us because we are "the rich Americans." No one else has money, and we were the only Americans they are involved with. Sometimes we could give it through the church, but they still would know it was us.

Alcoholism and Other Substance Abuse

Alcoholism is one of the worst problems here in Ukraine. In all grocery stores, there are several aisles of liquor, and people can get drunk very cheaply. Every day when I'm out, any time of day, I see drunks. Sometimes they're staggering by, or lying on the ground passed out. Some have been beat up the night before. In the different buildings we have lived in, we have known some of our alcoholic neighbors. They would act so differently when they were drunk; some nicer, some too friendly, while others would be a mean or disruptive.

One day Timmy was on his way home from our neighborhood grocery store and came across two children and their drunken father lying on the sidewalk. A little boy and his sister, who looked about twelve, were crying and pleading with their father to get up. She was crying, "Please Papa, please get up, we need you." They had been to the store and were carrying a few things, but the father finally collapsed. Timmy was able to talk to the children and offer his help. He got the dad up, put his arms around him and slowly walked him home. They lived in the apartment building right across the street from us. Timmy got them inside their apartment doorway, saw the kid's babushka, they said thank- you and he left.

This is a common thing here. It would be scary to think how many families go through this every day. I know this goes on in America as well, but I never was exposed to it. Now that I have seen how some people live, especially the children, I'm more thankful for the parents I have and realize how blessed I was to be raised in a Christian home.

Not only is the alcoholism bad, but people are killing themselves with cigarettes and drugs too. It seems like 99% of the population here smokes and the drug use is evident everywhere. I have seen bloody syringes in our stairwells and on the ground outside of our apartment. There are playgrounds around most of the apartments, and kids play there all the time, but I would be very fearful if I was a parent of small children. There is always broken glass around, which is bad enough, but I've seen syringes lying right in the playing area. People hang out there at night doing drugs and drop these dangerous objects right there.

We know missionaries who are specializing in this needy area. They have rehab and counseling centers ministering in different cities of Ukraine, but it's just a speck compared to the size of the problem. Pray that God will multiply their efforts.

Health and Healthcare

The Nazis and the Communists had already traumatized Ukraine forever, and then the Chernobyl Nuclear plant disaster occurred in 1986. Hadn't Ukraine been through enough already? Well, I just read (2008) that Ukraine has the fastest growing rate of AIDS. This is not just another disaster, but a great opportunity for believers to step up and minister to hurting people and a hurting nation. The Church in America and Ukraine hasn't been doing enough to help reach those with AIDS. I've heard of people here who have AIDS, being turned away from hospitals when they have needed medical assistance. One guy I heard about, a new believer had been critically hurt in some kind of accident and needed back surgery. He had a doctor who was willing to do the surgery, but the doctor couldn't find a hospital that would allow this man in as a patient.

During communism, medical care was free, if you can call it care. Now you have to pay for it. When I mean pay for it, I mean immediately, before you get cared for. We have had many a Ukrainian call needing money to pay for their appendectomy, as they're riding around in an ambulance with a ruptured appendix! Once our neighbor came running over saying one of her teenage daughter's teammates had been knocked out during handball, and they wouldn't x-ray her head until someone came up with thirty dollars! We're the only ones who had the money. This same neighbor herself was having surgery and came over crying saying that if they didn't pay the doctor an extra few hundred dollars that she just might **not** recover! Can you imagine playing with people's lives this way?

When I have visited Ukrainians in the hospital, I'm thankful I'm not sick and in a place like that. The typical hospital room usually has six or eight people in it. It can be coed too. One positive thing about so many in a room is that you have a good size audience when you're there visiting someone and have an opportunity to share the Gospel. They're all ears, with no place to go.

About these rooms: sometimes they have a sink, but usually the toilet is down the hall. The hallways have plaster missing from the walls and pot holes in the floors. At this particular place, I never saw a single person who looked like a doctor or nurse. There was no nurse's station, only a few pieces of dilapidated furniture sitting in the hall. If you're all alone, with no family or friends, I don't know what you do about food because you have to bring your own. Most of the time, the mattresses look awfully stained with who knows what on them; the sheets don't look much better. Now there are some nicer places for the rich Ukrainians to go, but I don't know anyone personally that has been to one of these facilities, since we don't have a single Ukrainian friend that is considered **even close** to having what a middle-class American has.

Dysfunctional Families

I thought the US had its problems, and it does, but Ukraine has a whole other level of dysfunctional situations that I've never heard of Americans experiencing. For example: one of our friends, who was a student in Kiev, would go to her hometown to visit her parents. When she would see them, not only was she visiting them, but also her father's mistress! Her father's mistress lived with them! Can you imagine these three people living together in a small apartment? What kind of example of marriage is this to our friend?

It seems like most of our friends have no father at home. Their parents either are divorced, or their father is gone; or he's a drunk that comes and goes, or they've never known him at all. I've heard of many couples who have been divorced for years but still have to live together, because they have no other place to go. We really see the affects of these fatherless Ukrainians; not knowing what a family is supposed to look like and not having male role models and leadership in the home. And if they are in the home, most of them aren't very good examples. Very few of our friends have had what we would consider a nurtured upbringing by two loving parents. I realize there are a lot of Americans in this same boat, but here their circumstances seem so much worse.

I feel so sorry for our friends who hate to go home. Some have to go home to one- room apartments where everyone sleeps in the same room, only to be awakened by their drunken father who comes stumbling in at 2:00 am and turns on the TV really loud. We knew one young woman, whose father wasn't mentally stable and wouldn't throw out any garbage. He kept it all in the apartment; it was waist deep and you just followed paths to get around from room to room. No wonder she never wanted to go home and stayed with people whenever she could.

Many of the Ukrainian households are made up of extended family members and the older children who have gotten married. Most newlyweds can't afford to live on their own; even to rent an apartment is now so expensive that they are forced to choose one of their parent's apartment to live in. Sometimes their grandparents live there along with their sibling who is divorced and has a kid; all this may be happening in a small, two- room apartment.

We've had friends ask us sometimes if they could come and just sit at our place. They would say, "It's so nice, like a dream." We know they aren't referring to the actual niceness of our apartment, but the atmosphere of our home. They've never experienced a Christian home, where parents love each other and children feel loved. For the first time they are exposed to a Christian home. If we've done nothing else but be an example of this, I think our mission has succeeded. We hope and pray now that those who have gotten saved can be the examples for their fellow countrymen as God teaches them.

CHAPTER 15

THIS WORLD IS NOT MY HOME

Being in another country, away from all you've known and become accustomed to, can feel lonely at times. As believers, it's comforting to know we're never alone. Jesus said He'd never leave us; He'd be with us to the end of the age. When you're in a situation where everything is different and sometimes confusing, it's great having God and His word that never changes. His presence in my life comforts me as I live in a culture that isn't as comfortable as my homeland. But I've learned now, that I shouldn't feel comfortable in Ukraine **or** America, because this world is not my home.

I often think of how Jesus must have felt. What a culture shock it must have been to leave Heaven and come to sinful earth! Heaven is my real home, so until I'm there, I should feel like an alien in any country. I'm not to get too comfortable; I'm just passing through.

In America, you can pretty much go through life and not see the needs of hurting people around you; especially when you live in a smaller town, and you don't use public transportation. You get in your car, go where you want to go; you don't have to get involved with anyone on the way. I know if you live in a city (especially in an inner city) the size of New York, Los Angeles, Detroit, etc. and ride public transportation, you will see a lot of needy people and heart breaking things similar to what I see here. But even the poorest people, in the most pitiful situations in America, have it better than a lot of people in other countries.

Don't Waste Your Life

You don't have to move to another country to be a missionary. You already are commissioned to be a missionary right where you live. Matthew 28:19-20 says, "Therefore go and make disciples of all nations, baptizing them in the name of the Father and of the Son and of the Holy Spirit, and teaching them to obey everything I have commanded you. And surely I am with you always, to the very end of the age."

You have your family, friends, neighbors, and people at work to share Christ with, and if you run out of these people, then you're more than welcome to join us here in Ukraine!

I would love to see every believer (my fellow American believers especially) get to go on a mission trip to a country less fortunate. It would do them a world of good to get out of their, "comfort zone." By-the-way, The United States of America is one big comfort zone, and if you don't agree, then you must not have ever left it.

I think any missionary reading this book would agree and many others too, but you really don't know how true it is unless you've lived some where less fortunate than America. If you've never gone on a mission trip of some kind, I challenge you to. If you can't leave America, do something locally like helping the needy people of your city or go to another state that has needs like the hurricane Katrina victims. There are many opportunities all around you. Do something that will stretch your faith. God wants to use you; let Him.

Many people are changed when they go on a mission trip; their prospective on life is never the same. But sadly, some only have it changed for a week or two, and then they get right back to the way they were before their trip. We're so easily distracted by what the world has to offer and the busyness of life, aren't we? We forget that God spoke to us. This happens all the time after people get back from a mission trip; they've been somewhere and served in some way and were a part of what the Lord was doing in a particular place. They leave all excited, but the devil doesn't want it to have a lasting impact, so the battle begins. In Luke 8:14-15 Jesus explains the parable about the seed which was sown on the different soils.

The seed that fell among thorns stands for those who hear, but as they go on their way they are choked by life's worries, riches and pleasures, and they do not mature. But the seed on good soil stands for those with a noble and good heart, who hear the word, retain it, and by persevering produce a crop.

Which soil do you want to describe your life? I hope I never get too busy to hear from the Lord. I don't want the world to choke out what God sows in my life. I want to produce fruit for His kingdom, don't you? I don't want to go through the day and not think about certain people that I'm in contact with and their spiritual condition. I want to live a life that is concerned about the lost world around me.

When I'm in America, I'm grieved by seeing lost people and the way they're living but, I'm also disappointed when I see what some believers are doing, or should I say not doing. There are some who claim to be believers, but I don't see that much of a difference in their lives. Christians are supposed to be different, but some believers just don't have enough fruit in their lives that show the world that Jesus is Lord of their lives. They spend their time and money just like everybody else. You can tell by their checkbook and watch what they do with their time, to see what other gods they have in their lives. I think it's harder to be a Christian in America because of the wealth and excess. We feel like we'll start seeing this in Kiev. The more prosperous it becomes, the less people will feel their need for God. Soon it may be that only those out in the smaller, more destitute cities will be more receptive. We've seen how the further west you go, and the more prosperous these countries get in Europe, then the colder these countries are toward the Gospel.

It seems like many Americans who fill up the pews on Sunday mornings are just hearers, not doers. I'm afraid that some believers have just become spectators who are taking part in a weekly, cultural event we call, "church." James 1:22-24 says,

Don't fool yourself into thinking that you are a listener when you are anything but, letting the Word go in one ear and out the other. Act on what you hear! Those who hear and don't act are like those who glance in the mirror, walk away, and two minutes later have no idea who they are, what they look like. (The Message)

I know most of you had heard this question, but ask yourself again "If everyone was doing what I'm doing, would the world be reached for Christ?" I know some people that can answer this question, "Yes," but it's not any where **near** enough. More believers have got to start **being The Church** to those around them. We only have a short time to live for God on this Earth, so please, don't waste your life. Live for God and others; I promise you'll have no regrets!

"For whoever wants to save his life will lose it, but whoever loses his life for me and for the gospel will save it."

Mark 8:35 (NIV)

CONTACT INFO

You may write Kenyon at kenyon.powers@gmail.com
Kenyon's website is http://powers.weebly.com

For more information on how to support and pray for the Powers ministry, go to http://www.gcmweb.org/getinvolved/Give.aspx

You can also learn more about Kenyon and her husband Timmy by going to their Facebook pages at:
Kenyon- http://www.facebook.com/profile.php?id=1405001128
Timmy- http://www.facebook.com/profile.php?id=519741405

Kiev Christian Academy is looking for Christian educators who would like to help fulfill the great commission by teaching missionary kids. For more information go to our website- www.kca.org.ua